The Legacy of the

Harry Potter Novels

Character Education

By Stefan Neilson
Joe and Nora Hutton

Illustrated by
Mark Bezenar

Aeon Hierophant Publishing
Financial and Personal Success, Inc

Seattle, WA USA * Harrison Hot Springs, B.C. Canada

The Legacy of the Harry Potter Novels

Character Education for Parents and Educators for the 21st Century

Vintage First Edition
Solid Platinum
Published by Aeon Hierophant
Financial and Personal Success, Inc.
P.O. Box 96, Mountlake Terrace WA 98043

Authors: Stefan Neilson, Joe Hutton, and Nora Hutton

Editors: Joe Hutton, Stefan Neilson, and Nora Hutton
Illustrated by Mark Bezenar

ISBN 1-880830-70-1
Library of Congress Card Number: 2001095699
Printed in the United States of America
Distributed by Financial and Personal Success, Inc.

Other Texts:
Personality Magic Booklet © 2001

For information write:

Financial and Personal Success, Inc.
P. O. Box 96
Mountlake Terrace, WA 98043 USA

Aeon Communications, Inc.
Thunderbird Estates, Box 100
Harrison Hot Springs, B.C.
Canada. V0M 1KO

(425) 672-8222
Web sites: financialsuccess.inc
winningcolors.com/harrypotter

e-mail: winningcolors@mindspring.com

Mind Map for Character Education

When you come to a fork in the road, take it! Yogi Berra

Good n' New

Personality Magic

- Celebrating Life
- Monsters-Under-the-Bed
- The Quest for Knowledge
- The Eternal Battle Between Good and Evil
- Authority Rides Amuck
- Become a Model Adventurer
- Child Abuse and Bullies
- False Judgments
- Captain Courageous
- The Spoiled Child
- Friendship

How to Be All You Can Be!

How to Begin to Identify and Change Behaviors with the Personality Magic Communication Cards

The Best Way to Process and Learn New Thoughts and Deal with Emotions: Inquire, Gather, Process and Apply.

Why not use 21st Century Behavioral Character Change Tools?

Acknowledgments

J. K. Rowling: The author of the Harry Potter novels, whose imaginative genius has inspired the minds and hearts of the world's youth and enticed millions of adults to revisit the captivating world they once inhabited.

Steven E. Dunn: Who inspired me with his live presentations and whose format, Inquire, Gather, Process and Apply is used as the basis for each lesson. The format may be found in their text: Williams, Bruce R., & Dunn, Steven E. 2000. *Brain Compatible Learning for the Block.* Arlington Heights, IL: Skylight Training and Publishing, Inc.

Laurence Martel, Ph. D.: Who is sharing the wisdom of his mind and heart with millions of others through his workshops and written articles. Included in this text: Learning Styles Map, Good-n-New exercises. Such phrases as "Stupidity is a Learned Behavior" have been integrated in the chapter exercises.

Elizabeth Schriever: Who inspired the NEFE (National Endowment for Financial Education) High School Financial Planning Program text, which served as a model for us in the effective use of the Steven E. Dunn paradigm.

JROTC Curriculum Designers: Who first brought my attention to the interest of youth in Harry Potter and the works of Laurence Martel, Ph.D., and Steven E. Dunn.

Pat Rimstad: Who is an 84-year-old great grandmother. She is excited about life with 5 children, 21 grand children and 28 great grandchildren and still shares the magic of her tales with them.

Harrison Hot Springs, B. C., Canada, 2001 Sand Sculpturing Competition: Photos of sand creations that take us to the castles of the imagination.

The Consultants: Alexandra, Kylie, Jacob, Josh, Shannon, Nathan and Matthew Hutton, Harry Potter fans whose assistance in the development of the material in this text is sincerely appreciated

Mark Bezenar

The above "mindkey" illustration
is symbolic of a person's quest
to find the key to his and her own mind
that will unlock his and her potential.
As with Harry Potter at the outset,
many people are not aware
of the power and potential they possess.
Much of the struggle, enchantment and reward in life
are related to this search for
personal power, understanding and awareness.

About the Authors

Stefan Neilson, M.A.

Stefan was graduated in psychology from Columbia University, New York. As an author, instructor of upper management and university professor, Stefan uses his twelve years of university training as a consultant, seminar and convention director.
His expertise includes consulting, communication, keynotes, counseling, teaching, and radio and television interviews. Seminars and keynotes have included such clients as McDonald's, National Management Association, General Dynamics, JROTC (Junior Reserve Officer Training Corps) and various school districts throughout the nation. Stefan was Director of Counseling and Guidance for a dozen high schools and is presently the president and CEO of Aeon Communications, Inc. USA and Canada and Financial and Personal Success, Inc. Over 150,000 students in 1,500 schools are participating in the Communication Behavioral Identification process called Winning Colors® created by Stefan Neilson and illustrated by Shay Thoelke.

Joe Hutton

A professional accountant, Joe has had a rich and interesting career, including being a football coach, University instructor, public practitioner and businessman. In these varied occupations, he has seen the need for a program such as Winning Colors© Personality Magic and has applied the program in business organizations, with dramatic results. He is also one of the legions who feel that the Harry Potter books by J. K Rowling are nothing short of marvelous!

Nora Hutton

Nora is a professional mother. With the birth of the first of her five children, she decided that there was no greater calling than nurturing young minds and hearts into successful and productive adults. After more than 40 years of marriage to her husband Joe, her family, which now includes seven grandchildren, is ample tribute to the fact that her decision was the right one. A dedicated fan of Winning Colors© Personality Magic, she shares some of the stories and insights, which may lead others to careers which will be as rewarding as her own.

Mark Bezenar

Mark Bezenar gives new meaning to the term "Renaissance Man". Born in Edmonton, Alberta in 1965, he is a former champion athlete. He is an accomplished artist, writer, musician and inventor. With new technologies emerging, Mark is poised to start his own multi-media corporation.

Legend has it that an Indian Chief
was counseling a young brave.
The Chief told the young man that
each of us has an angry dog and
a gentle dog within us.
The young brave asked the Chief:
"What is the strongest in you?"
The chief replied:
"The one I feed the most!"
-Native American Wisdom
Mark Bezenar

Contents

The Legacy of the Harry Potter Novels

Character Education for Parents and Educators for the 21st Century

The other day I was told of parents of a young boy who, because they cared, became concerned because of their son's preoccupation with the adventures of Harry Potter. Although only eight years old, the boy had read every one of J.K. Rowling's captivating novels several times. To divert his attention, their strategy was to take all the books and paraphernalia concerning Harry Potter away from him. They felt that any further contact with Harry Potter could have a negative effect on his mental and spiritual development. What a tragedy!

Somehow they had forgotten how, when they were young and their imaginations were rampant, the frightening witch in Cinderella; the deceptive fox in Pinocchio; the vicious wolf in Little Red Riding Hood and the comic books galore, starring Batman, Wonder Woman and Superman. Somehow they had forgotten how their parents, friends or baby sitters had sat and read one of these fantasies to them before they went to sleep. They may have lived with an imaginary, invisible character that they consulted on a regular basis.

My cousin lived in constant contact with a "Mrs. Shooby" who never failed to advise her on the important things in life.

I had a corner of a blanket that always soothed me and gave me a sense of security as a child. My parents noticed this and would take that corner and put it at the bottom of the bed. I would pull the blanket around until I found that secure corner. Thank goodness they did not take the blanket away from me.

Somehow they had forgotten their introduction to the eternal struggle between good and evil. They had forgotten the lessons they learned from these imaginings, called eidetic imagery.

They had forgotten how their imaginations were freed to allow them to become all they ever wanted to be in life.

Unfortunately, many parents, unmindful of the importance of such elements in the growing up process, discourage this fantasy world of Santa Clauses, Mrs. Shoobys and secure corner of the blanket. The development of this creative part of the mind is held back and their children are left on the ground, unable to soar to see all that might be.

This text is a practical manual meant for those parents and educators who still believe that there is a tooth fairy and a pot of gold at the end of the rainbow and want youth to find it. They recognize that a vibrant imagination is the very soul of creativity. They see that through the trials and tribulations of a Harry Potter, young minds will find it, guided along the way like Albus Dumbledore does as a mentor for Harry. They will leave their children with the Harry Potter Legacy.

Considerations

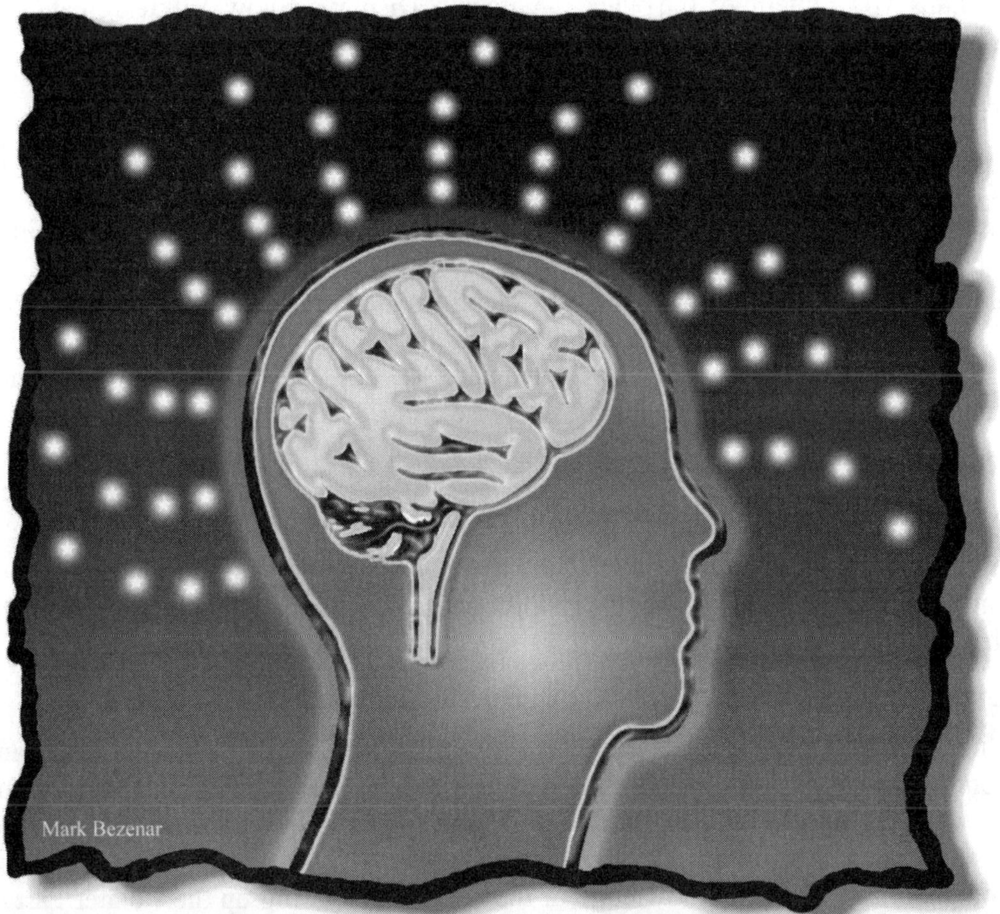

Parents:

1) Although the manual is designed for group interaction, you may adapt the majority of the thoughts and exercises to a one-on-one basis.
2) The lessons may be taken in any order. It is important that you choose which lesson you consider the most important for your situation.

The power and role of the Story is our entrance to a:

1) person's thinking
2) person's feelings
3) person's imagination
4) model of right and wrong behavior
5) vehicle for sharing and connecting people of all ages
6) lasting memory impression
7) forum for distinguishing between Good and Evil
8) method for our children to teach and tell stories to their peers.

A note about Terror and the imagination of children.

"The imagination is more important than knowledge." Albert Einstein

Perhaps you remember the wicked witch in Disney's Snow White (created by adults for "children")? How many children remembered the images flashed on the screen in their nightmares? Did you hide under the bed, too?
The movie "The Shining" is no less scary than the subtle way children have been scared through "general audience" film categorization and brutal cartoons. The images conjured up by characters like Fagan in Charles Dickens' ***Oliver Twist*** as well as those in ***Harry Potter and the Sorcerer's Stone*** (Voldemort) sometimes leave the child terrified.
This manual is designed for the conscientious parents and educators who love their children enough to help them deal with the "monsters under the bed." Acting out and debriefing the child, as the exercises do, causes both a mental and emotional understanding and catharsis in the child.

Character

Note the word "act" is contained within the word character.

In this manual, character is used as the manner of distinguishing between "good" and "evil". Aristotle's principle of a prudent person is that right reason rules the thing to be done. The objective is to raise a child with an ability to act justly.

Understanding Diversity (The four genies in a bottle.)

Understanding Diversity is how we optimize the way we think, feel and communicate with others and ourselves. Sometimes we want to create and think, so we bring up the Planner Part of Self; at other times we want to lead and get results, so we bring up the Builder Part of Self; at other times, we want companionship and the knowledge of the heart, so we bring up the Relater Part of Self: at still other times, we want action, fun and excitement so we bring up the Adventurer Part of Self.

Think of the Native American story of the angry and gentle dog inside and how the strongest is the one fed the most. Taking that a step further, think of us as having four genies in our Aladdin's Lamp. Which one is the strongest? The one we "Rub" the most.

Conflict

Conflict happens when these four parts of self are in conflict with those of others and even within us.

For a more extensive explanation and application of the above, contact:
Dr. Laurence Martel, Intellearn, P.O. Box 5784 Hilton Head Island, SC 29938.
Telephone (843) 686-4050

Be All You Can Be!

Below are the objectives of this hands-on text

Character Education: The Legacy of Harry Potter
helps youth acquire behaviors that build solid Character.

How to get along with others

- How to use the Winning Colors® cards and four phrase chapter plan to understand self and others
- How to make others feel cool when they are with you
- How to make people think you're great
- How to develop people skills in order to achieve your goals
- How to make anyone comfortable with you.
- How to let others know they can trust you
- How to get others to like you
- How to get your ideas across to teachers, parents and other kids
- How to build a strong team
- How to feel good about yourself and be part of a winning team

Power: What it is! How to get it!

- How to become a powerful leader
- How to gain power and the respect of others
- How to understand how people think and feel
- How to lessen anger and hostility toward you
- How to motivate yourself and others
- The importance of friendship, what it is and how to get it
- How to use your mind and heart to get what you want
- How to be a winner

How To Begin

In order to communicate successfully with others, one must have knowledge of her or his present behavioral communication strengths. A quick and easy card sort may assess these, as follows:
Take the four colored cards and place them in the formation of a clock.

Check out your present behavioral strengths
with the Winning Colors® Personality Magic identification cards.

Clockwork green, brown, blue and red!

1. Place the four colored cards before you like a clock, illustrations up, in any order. Place one at the 12 o'clock position, the next at the 3 o'clock position, the next at the 6 o'clock position and the last card at the 9 o'clock position.

Sample

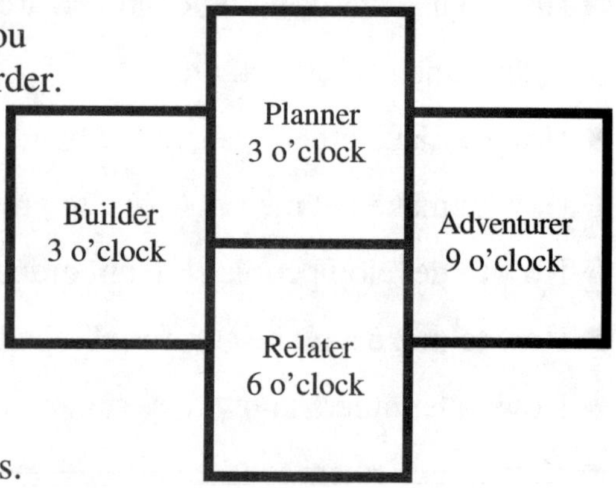

2. Read the words, look at the illustrations.

Now Ask Yourself This Question: Which Card Is Truly Like Me?
Which Card Is My Strongest Behavioral Strength?

3. Based on your own internal feelings and thoughts (not what you think, or feel that others expect of you), rearrange the cards by placing the card that best describes you at the 12 o'clock position; the next at the 3 o'clock position; the next at the 6 o'clock position and the weakest at the 9 o'clock position.

Sample

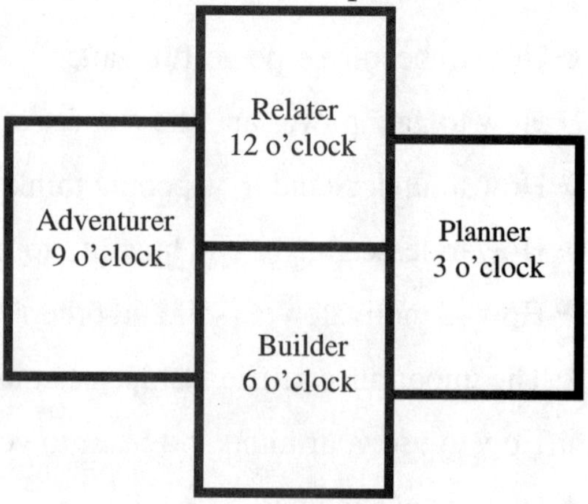

4. Assign numbers to the colored cards, based on the ranking you just made, with #1 the closest match which is at the 12 o'clock position, #4 the poorest match which you placed at the 9 o'clock position.

READ the back of the card you chose as #1.
Is this like you?
If not, go through the cards again, making new choices.

Sample of one person's selection.

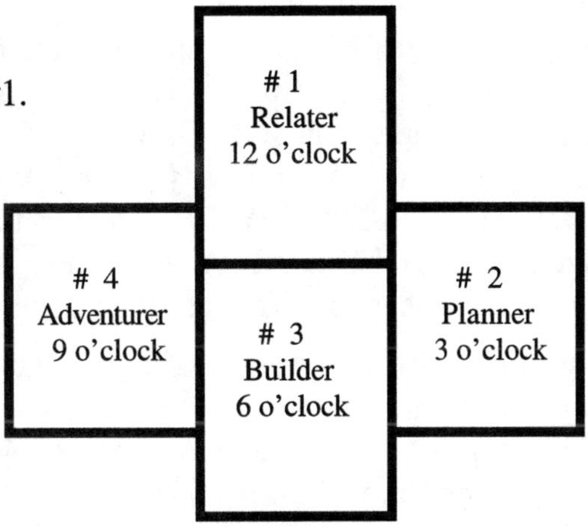

5. Indicate below, the order in which YOU sorted your cards (1-4) as the sample above:

☐ PLANNER or FOX PART OF ME (GREEN)

☐ BUILDER or BULL/BEAR PART OF ME (BROWN)

☐ RELATER or DOLPHIN PART OF ME (BLUE)

☐ ADVENTURER or TIGER PART OF ME (RED)

The above gives you a thumbnail sketch of your own behavioral communication strengths.

REMEMBER: These are the four parts of yourself. You are all four. In most cases, one cluster of behaviors may be stronger than another.
The goal of Winning Colors® is to be able to bring up different behaviors, according to the situation.

The order of the cards indicates your present comfort zone and primary communication behaviors.

Personality Magic Communication Cards

How to interpret the significance of your choice.

Your Secret to Present Main Thinking Priorities and the Motivation of others.

The Personality Magic communication cards are tools that will assist you in identifying both your own and other's present thoughts, reasons for action and major communication style. The cards the person places first and second indicate the person's main way of communicating. **FOR EFFECTIVE COMMUNICATION WITH ANYONE, YOU MUST "PLUG IN" TO THAT WAY OF COMMUNICATING.** For successful relationships, there must be "different strokes for different folks" depending **ALWAYS** on the situation.

Sometimes your observation skills of both your own way of communication and the ways other communicate may need improvement. The Personality Magic card process will help you communicate more successfully with friends, teachers, family members, managers and even with complete strangers. There are **various memory hooks** that will help you remember the best communication approach to take with anyone.

When a person places one of following cards at the 12 o'clock position, you will immediately know their central thought patterns.

Planner Card (Ideas will predominate)

Thinking/Creative Part of Self: The Color Green represents the mysterious depths of the oceans
Animal: As clever as a Fox.
Illustrations that act as magnets for persons with Planner strengths
Words that attract people with strong Planner behaviors

Builder Card (Leadership will predominate)

Leadership Part of Self: The Color Brown represents the solid foundation of the earth
Animals: Bull and Bear the symbols of strength and power.
Illustrations that act as magnets for persons with Builder strengths
Words that attract people with strong Builder behaviors

Relater Card (Relationships with others will predominate)

Team Building Part of Self: The Color Blue is like the openness of the sky
Animal: Dolphins the symbols of working together and supporting each other
Illustrations that are magnets for persons with Relater strengths
Words that attract people with strong Relater behaviors

Adventurer Card (Action will predominate)

Action Part of Self: The Color Red is like fire
Animal: "Hold that Tiger"; walk the walk rather than just talking the talk.
Illustrations that act as magnets for persons with Adventurer strengths
Words that attract people with strong Adventurer behaviors

Planner
Build an Atmosphere of Freedom of Thought

If a person chooses the Planner card first, the following is usually true.

Comfort zone: Open to new and creative ideas - abstract thinking - the latest and most innovative procedures and product - prefers creative subject input that challenges the mind – needs quiet time - abhors triviality - not too concerned about dress, hair style or exterior details - future oriented (visionary) - interested in science fiction and exploration of space - revolutionary – empathetic.

Demands on people: Creative thinking - work alone - develop the mind and reasoning process - be logical - long and detailed explanations, reports and meetings.

Your secret vocabulary for developing Planner behaviors and getting along with persons with strong **Planner** behaviors:

* think * understand * discover * perfect * correct * listen * plan * new ways *
* predict * inner life * change * mystery * cause * invent * exactness * improve *

How to build powerful teams, self-esteem, success, maximize productivity in others and reinforce leadership.

*** PERSONALITY MAGIC'S HOT BUTTONS ***

When the **Planner or Fox (green)** part of you is very strong, consider what motivates you and apply it.

- Take a serious approach to Planners' communications ...
- Take a thoughtful, calm, cool and collected interest. Don't dominate with your ideas ...
- Practice patience, allow and encourage personal creativity ...
- Design work that allows three times longer to complete than the Builder would ...
- Note that time constraints limit the creativity of the Planner ...
- Give ample warning before calling on them to speak in public ...
- When asking for comments at meetings, do not call on Planners first. They need more time to consider their response ...
- Giving harsh bottom-line treatment causes withdrawal or feelings of inadequacy and unsatisfactory work ...

If a person chooses the Builder card first, the following is usually true.

Comfort zone: Orderly, structured procedures at work, home, school, social, recreation - pride in organization, school, family - preference for input and procedures that have a solid, traditional, stable foundation - importance of discipline, routine - desk in position of authority - conservative dress and hairstyles - everything must indicate status, e. g., home, family, clubs.

Demands on people: Duty conscious - obedient, respectful, success oriented, hard working, reliable, prepared, responsible - able to finish projects and assignments within time limits - reports must be neat, concise and on time.

Your secret vocabulary for developing Builder behaviors and getting along with persons with strong **BUILDER** behaviors:

* organized * law and order * power * saving * results * honor *
* track record * duty * responsibility * * accountability * bottom-line *
* prepared * building * clear-cut * authority * leading * status *

How to build powerful teams, self-esteem, success, maximize productivity in others and reinforce leadership

* PERSONALITY MAGIC'S HOT BUTTONS *

When the **Builder or Bull and Bear (brown)** part of you is very strong, consider what motivates you and apply it.

- Take a bottom-line approach to other Builders' communication …
- Be duty conscious and comfortable with rules and directions …
- Assign accountable and responsible positions according to talents …
- Explain directions in a step-by-step, concrete fashion ...
- Treat others in the right and proper way ...
- Give them status or control over people or things according to their people skills ...
- Have an understandable reward system ...
- Establish a stable, structured, home/social/work situation ...
- Let them know what is expected of them and have a concrete reward system ...
- Establish daily routines and give step-by-step, concise explanations ...
- Never embarrass or cause them to lose face in front of their peers ...

Relater: Friendly Personal Interactions

If a person chooses the Relater card first, the following is usually true.

Comfort zone: Supportive, friendly atmosphere - emotions are crucial - people focused - slogans and posters - harmonious home and teamwork - vocal exchanges such as discussion groups - wants people to like him or her - prefers procedures that are people centered and humanistic - importance of friendliness, sharing - makes self accessible for personal as well as work needs of people - bright well colored, coordinated dress.

Demands on people: Share ideas and feelings, enthusiasm, harmony - speak out in meetings and at home - emotional appreciation - emphasis on exterior detail, such as how the report looks, how people are dressed.

Your secret vocabulary for developing Relater behaviors for getting along with persons with strong **RELATER** behaviors:

* friendly * harmony * people-centered * exterior detail * togetherness * group *
* love * being accepted * giving * honest feelings * teamwork * romantic *

How to build powerful teams, self-esteem, success, maximize productivity in others and reinforce leadership.

* PERSONALITY MAGIC'S HOT BUTTONS *

When the **Relater or Dolphin (blue)** part of you is very strong, consider what motivates you and apply it.

* Take a friendly approach to other Relaters' communication ...
* Provide a social atmosphere and occasions for them to interact ...
* Respect other Relaters' feelings by not imposing your feelings on them ...
* Give genuine concern, a smile, and a kind word and do not dominate the conversation ...
* Allow them time to talk with their friends such as discussion groups ...
* Give occasions for emotional outlets and freedom of their personal expression ...
* Smile when passing and congratulate them on various occasions especially when they least expect it ...

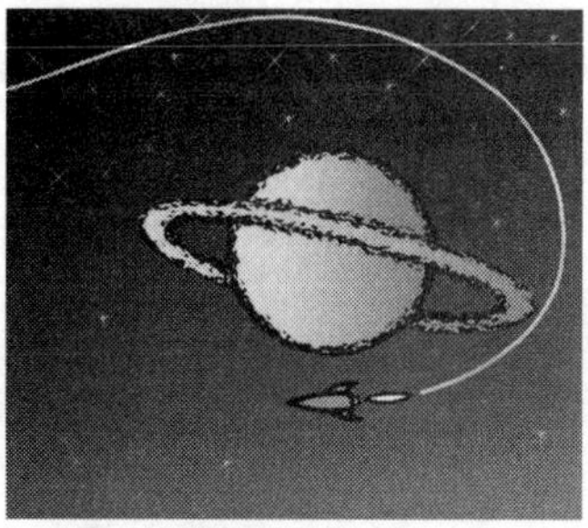

Adventurer
Build an Atmosphere of Action and Excitement

If a person chooses the Adventurer card first, the following is usually true.

Comfort zone: Action, unstructured work situations - movers - prefers procedures that are useful, dynamic, practical and hands-on - importance of spontaneity - here and now are important - be on stage – learning style is touch

Demands on others: Action oriented - spontaneous responses - respond quickly to changes - be competitive - be on stage at a moments notice - pick up the pieces - fun and light-hearted attitude - take a joke

Your secret vocabulary for developing Adventurer behaviors for getting along with persons with strong **ADVENTURER** behaviors:
* fun * excitement * spend * adventure * spontaneous * action * machines *
* gamble * fun * chance * games * fast * change * act out * joke * entrepreneur *

How to build powerful teams, self-esteem, success, maximize productivity in others and reinforce leadership.

*** PERSONALITY MAGIC'S HOT BUTTONS ***

When the **Adventurer or Tiger (red)** part of you is very strong, consider what motivates you and apply it.

- Take a light-hearted, fun or action approach to Adventurers' communications
- Speak to the here and now ...
- Be as flexible as they are to changing action; be careful of the action's direction ...
- Direct spontaneous action towards positive goals; celebrate your wins and let them be one of the major sources for discouraging turnover, delinquency or criminal actions ...
- Involve them in any positive action situation. Be careful not to get caught in the thrill...
- Create result-oriented action situations according to the family, club's, company's or organization's goals ...
- Allow them to play a "starring" role on any occasion possible ...
- Check and make sure they are in positive action situations, provide exercise areas and home, work, recreational or social occasions to let off steam ...
- With younger tigers, control is needed but do it warmly and lovingly ...

The Four-Phase Lesson Plan:
How It Applies to The Legacy of Harry Potter Novels

Each of the following lessons deals with a particular type of behavior that is experienced frequently by children and adults alike. In the Harry Potter novel, many behaviors are demonstrated, some in normal situations and some in outrageous, imaginative circumstances. In order to present each type of behavior in a meaningful way, the chapter relates to Harry Potter's experiences to develop the theme. As an aid to the exploration of ideas, each chapter is broken down into four phases: **inquire, gather, process** and **apply.**

Student Groups:

INQUIRE Phase: Students share and communicate what they already know about the theme. They examine their own memories and experiences. They share with each other what they already know. They also evaluate their attitudes, feelings and motivation about their relationship with themselves and with others.

GATHER Phase: The Students investigate and discover new information about the effect that successful, positive communication can have when applied to the behavior being examined. In a nutshell, this is the stage when research skills are learned that will be of value throughout life when they face challenges. They will, at least, know where to begin by using the Winning Colors® Process. This process is also used as a framework to build on, helping the youths evaluate their present behavioral communication strengths. Activities at this stage connect newly discovered information, in this case as found in the experiences of Harry Potter, those of the authors and those of the instructor. Combined with what the students already know about getting along well with others, they begin building characteristics of excellence and self-esteem.

PROCESS Phase: The youths are given the opportunity to practice what they have learned in a safe environment, with a facilitator. They learn to assimilate all the information from the Inquire and Gather phases by using and acting upon it. The Winning Colors behavioral clusters will assist them in this phase as they discover why people act the way they do and what to do about it. For instance, the process of developing the Relater Part of self (Lesson 2) can be achieved by placing one youth in the center of the group. Each of the others in the circle bombards her or him with positive remarks. Activities in this phase become "hands-on" in the sense of practicing characteristics of excellence.

APPLY Phase: The participants now have the competence to transfer what they have learned about positive communication to their personal lives. The bottom-line is that these behaviors learned and experienced in a controlled situation may be applied to activities in everyday situations. It would be profitable to meet later and discuss the students' successes in the application of what they have learned in this process, sharing their real life experiences.

The Power of the "Good-n-New", used throughout the Lessons

Integrative Learning Teaching Strategies *

Using the process of "Good-n-New" provides an excellent opportunity to set a tone of positive thinking for the rest of the day. This enhances opportunities for productive experiences. Emphasizing the good in our lives reduces stress and allows our energy to focus on finding solutions to challenges or completing tasks. The good and new may be seen as a therapeutic cleansing or stabilizing strategy. It provides an avenue to give one self - recognition for having provided something positive for oneself and for others. The idea of expressing something that has happened to you may start out as a simple act, but when you are talking about it to someone else, it can take on a more meaningful aspect. The fact of going home and having dinner with your family can seem more important as a result. In short, this exercise is a good stimulus to shape a positive self-image.

Objective: The participants will be able to demonstrate their feelings about something good and new that happened to them recently. The purpose is for people in a group to feel good about themselves.

Having each participant personally tell a large or small group his or her recent good experience helps to create an atmosphere that is positive and supportive in the classroom. This allows one to search her or his life for a short period of time and to come up with something that makes her or him feel worthy. The good and new allows time for sharing and is great for a warm-up exercise. It also provides an opportunity for a non-verbal person to speak in a small group, when otherwise she or he might not do so. Further, we may associate this practice with the idea of "Give to the world the best that you have, and the best will come back to you." A positive attitude and an enriching environment are key attributes of the climate of accelerated learning.

Method: The instructor or group leader announces that it is time for today's "Good-n-New". Each person who would like to speak stands and gives a short narrative of his or her good experience that took place in the past twenty-four hours. In this case, the "Good-n-New" is given at the end of the Learning Activity.

The good and new is a valuable way of beginning or ending a class, because it offers a positive way of enriching self-esteem for the individual and the group. It also creates an attitude of learning expectancy. This exercise helps everyone to turn attention away from the negative thoughts within themselves and those that bombard them from without. In a very real sense it is transforming.

* Dr. Laurence D. Martel, President of Integrative Learning Systems, Inc., and the National Academy of Integrative Learning.

Introduction - Historic Literary Significance of Harry Potter

The Fantasy of the 21st Century

Begin by having the youth sort the Personality Magic Cards. There are elementary cards and a text "Here's looking at you Kid!" for kindergarten and younger children available. Refer to Bibliography.

Next, have the group read J. K. Rowling's "***Harry Potter and the Sorcerer's Stone***" or listen to the tapes available at bookstores.
For younger folk, it is suggested that the parent or educator read the story. After a section when the author has made a significant point, ask the young person what this means to her or him. Follow the process of Inquiry, Gather, Process and Apply as set out above. In the following lessons, certain behaviors and ideas will be highlighted that might be a source of sharing your world with the students.

"***Harry Potter and the Sorcerer's Stone***", as the rest of the series, brings to mind the beginnings of English literature with the 10th century poem, Beowulf: a hero who wounds the monster Grendel. He pursues Grendel's mother, a witch, to her cave where he beheads both Grendel and the witch. Those cognizant of the early morality plays will recognize the "sermons" to Harry by Dumbledore, just in case the reader has missed the message. You may also compare the "good and evil" character development of the Potter novels to those of Chaucer and Shakespeare. Of course Dumbledore is the reincarnation of a much more positive and constructive Merlin.

It is said of T. S. Eliot, that he was asked what his poem "The Wasteland" meant: Mr. Eliot asked the inquisitor what he thought the significance of the poem was. The gentleman went on for some time replying. Mr. Eliot then responded: "That is what I meant!"

If this text is to be of value to the Youth, it is CRUCIAL that they discover what the experiences and story of Harry Potter mean to them, NOT to YOU! This is a delicate task for any parent or educator, as there is a strong tendency to skip this important step in the creative education process. There is an urge to lead rather than guide. Many adults have learned not to learn. This is why in each lesson there is an "INQUIRE" stage, which attends to what the youth's present knowledge of the subject is. It is only then that new information is brought in through a "GATHERING" stage.

To augment the learning process, the four parts of self, through the **Personality Magic Cards** is the practical application. It shows the educator or parent **HOW TO** help the students or youths communicate and grow as successful persons. This practical application will flow through each lesson.

A summary of the crucial aspects of this text:

* In order to put to rest fears of negative consequences for young people reading *Harry Potter*, instructors and parents are shown how to use Harry Potter as a hands-on aid for positive character behavioral development.

* Present behaviors of both self and others are identified through the Personality Magic cards as instruments for measuring behavioral change.

* A lesson format of Inquire, Gather, Process and Apply is employed in order to have maximum understanding and positive results.

* Personal Empowerment Statements are given as models. The participants are encouraged to develop and write out their own. Place them on small cards, repeating them with imagination and feeling often, until the desired goal is attained.

* It is not necessary to follow lesson by lesson. Pick those lessons most appropriate for your situation.

* Group activities that are specified for one section of a lesson may be applicable to other lessons, such as the conversation circles, i.e., two circles are formed with students facing each other and discussing ideas that arise from the unit.

* If you are using this text on a one-on-one basis, select those exercises and materials applicable and relevant to your situation.

* At the end of each lesson there is space provided for your notes and reflections. You may also use the blank left side of the page for your personal remarks.

Notes and Reflections:

Personality Magic

Mark Bezenar

Personal Notes and Reflections

Lesson One

Personality Magic

Phase 1 -- Inquire:

Supplies:

1) Chart paper and markers

Direct the Focus (Objective):

Discover what the students already know about themselves and what is the best way for them to communicate with others.

Learning Activities:

The instructor facilitates:

1) Have each person write out a short biographical history of his or her life.
2) Divide the class into teams of four. Have each group identify people and situations that cause them to have difficulty in communicating.
3) Why is one type of person likeable and not another?
4) Ask the groups to list the behaviors that turn them off.
5) Ask them to list the behaviors that they like in others.
6) Each person, who would like to speak, stands and gives a narrative of his or her "Good-n-New" experience that took place during these activities.
7) Have the teams record their insights on the chart paper. Each team reports its findings back to the group. Put the results up on the wall.

Reflection:

1) The "Good-n-New" for me is ______________________________.
2) I learned the following about myself ______________________________.

Personal Empowerment Statement:

I find it easy and enjoyable to relate to new people I choose to get to know better.

Phase 2 -- Gather:

Supplies:

1) Personality Magic Cards
2) Chart paper and markers
3) ***Harry Potter and the Sorcerer's Stone***

Direct the Focus (Objective):

Have the students become aware that there are "different strokes for different folks".

Learning Activities

The instructor facilitates:

A Story for Discussion

Legend has it that there existed a mysterious country, "The Valley of the Blind", in the wildest wastes of Ecuador's Andes. An old proverb stated: "In the Country of the Blind, The One-eyed Man is King." Nunez went in search of this legendary country. After many years of searching, by accident, he fell down a crevasse and found it and, indeed, all the residents were blind.

He told the inhabitants of the wonders of sight, but they did not believe him. He was treated as the village fool. In due course, he fell in love with the daughter of the chief, Medina-sarote. The requirement for marriage set by the chief was that Nunez must have those ugly projections be operated on and taken out, so he could rise to the level of the blind citizen. He agreed: as the saying goes: "Love is blind!"

On the day of the operation, Nunez noticed the rocks above the village were coming loose and were about to come cascading down on the village. He ran through the village warning the citizens of what he saw. Their response was that Nunez had once again gone mad. They tried to catch him, but he escaped up the mountainside. As he looked back, he saw the blind citizens racing to and fro, attempting to find him and take out those horrible eyes of his. Then the rocks came tumbling down the mountain. The village disappeared in the dust.

H.G. Wells, *The Country of the Blind*

Consider at least one lesson to be drawn from this fable: Putting aside your values (your gift of sight), to join the mob or gang. The Personality Magic Cards are eye-openers, so you come to understand, in practical terms, the truism: "Different Strokes for Different Folk."

1) Have the students sort the cards according to the instructions given on pages 12 through 16. Follow the instructions exactly. This procedure is crucial if the participants are to fully understand the significance of knowing both their own behavioral strengths and those of others.
2) To reinforce the sorting process, have the group participate in the "Guessing Game". Have them guess not only how their peers sort the cards but the instructor as well.
3) After the Guessing Game, have the students check out their guesses. At the very beginning, the youths may put the brown card (authority figure) at the 12 o'clock position because the instructor is in a position of authority. With practice, they will be able to read between the lines and realize this may not be their strength, but their behaviors in the situation.
4) Have them practice having others sort the cards. You must make sure that they have the participants place the cards **FACE UP, IN THE FORMATION OF A CLOCK, AND ACCORDING TO WHAT IS MOST**

LIKE THEM (not how they act on the job or how they would like to be!) Emphasize over and over again, that the card sort is a description of himself or herself at the **PRESENT** time and that all four behavioral groups are integral parts of their whole personality. Point out that, at different times in their lives or in different situations, another card may be their strongest. **THE MAIN OBJECTIVE OF PERSONALITY MAGIC IS THE SELF-EMPOWERMENT TO BRING UP THE BEHAVIORS REQUIRED BY THE SITUATION!**

4) Each person, who would like to speak, stands and gives a narrative of his or her "Good-n-New" experience that took place during these activities.
5) Have the teams record their observations on chart paper and report the results to the whole group. Post the charts on the wall for all to see.

Wisdom of the Wizards of the World:

They be blind leaders of the blind.
And if the blind lead the blind, both shall fall into the ditch.

Matthew, 15, 14

Reflection:

1) I learned the following about myself in the card sort ____________________.
2) I learned the following about others in the card sort ____________________.
3) The best way to have a successful group or team is: ____________________.

Personal Empowerment Statement:

I take great pride in bringing up the Planner, Builder, Relater or Adventurer part of me according to the situation (name the situation and the part of self to bring up for success). When communicating with (name the person) it is better for me to bring up (name the part of self) to best communicate with her or him.

Phase 3 -- Process:

Supplies:

1) Personality Magic Cards
2) Chart paper and markers
3) ***Harry Potter and the Sorcerer's Stone***

Direct the Focus (Objective):

The students learn specific behaviors and strategies for successfully communicating with others.

Learning Activities

The instructor facilitates:

A Story for Discussion

Since developing the concept of Winning Colors© and presenting it to people of all ages across the world, I have found that it has proven to be both simple and profound. The clusters of behaviors represented by the colors and cards are quickly grasped, while the opportunities for understanding and effective communication expand with each use. With experience, each person we encounter brings to mind one or more of the four colors and, with them, all of the key words, hot buttons and reactions we need for successful communication.

" Practice maketh perfection"

Proverbs

1) Break the class into teams of four. Have each team made up of the same behavioral strengths: Planners in one group, Builders in another, and so on. It may be necessary to take the second or even the third strength (color) to make the foursome, if the overall group tends to be skewed to certain behaviors.
2) Give them an assignment: List at least 6 to 8 characteristics of the perfect school.
3) Have the teams record their insights on the chart paper. Each team reports the results back to the group. Put the resulting charts up on the wall.
4) Next, sort the students into different groups of four. Have each behavioral strength (Color) represented, as clearly as possible, in each team: a Planner, a Builder, a Relater and an Adventurer. It may be necessary to take the second or even the third strength (color) to make the foursome if the overall class tends to be skewed to certain behaviors.
5) Give them an assignment: List at least 6-8 characteristics of a perfect family. Contrast these characteristics with several of the Dursley's (Chapter One).
6) Have the teams record their insights on the chart paper. Each team reports the results back to the group. Put the resulting charts up on the wall.
7) Assemble the entire class. Place two chart sheets in view of all. On the first chart sheet place the words "Groups made up of the same behavioral strengths." Divide the chart in two with the headings: "Advantages" and "Disadvantages". Have the students state their views.
8) On the next chart sheet place the words: "Groups made up of different behavioral strengths." Divide the chart in two with the headings: "Advantages" and "Disadvantages", as above. Have the students state their views. Compare the results.
9) Divide the group into pairs. Partners take turns interviewing each other to determine their level of understanding of the Personality Magic cards.
10) Each person, who would like to speak, stands and gives a narrative of his or her "Good-n-New" experience that took place during these activities.
11) Have the teams record their observations on chart paper and report the results to the whole group. Post the charts on the wall for all to see.

Wisdom of the Wizards of the World:

There's none so blind as those who will not see.

Proverb

Reflection:

1) The Good-n-New for me is ________________________________.

2) The different values of the Planner are ________________________________.

3) The different values of the Builder are ________________________________.

4) The different values of the Relater are ________________________________.

5) The different values of the Adventurer are ____________________________.

Personal Empowerment Statement:

I find it an exciting challenge in discovering the behavioral strengths of others and bringing up those parts of myself that will make me successful.

⚒ Phase 4: -- Apply:

Supplies:

1) Personality Magic Cards
2) Chart paper and markers
3) ***Harry Potter and the Sorcerer's Stone***

Direct the Focus (Objective):

Empower the students to know how to bring up the crucial part of self for the situation.

Learning Activities:

Instructor facilitates:

A Story for Discussion

Following a recent presentation of the Winning Colors® Program to a group of car salespeople, one of the participants told me how important the newly acquired skills were in avoiding getting off on the wrong foot with a potential buyer. " If I see they are showing Green (Planner) behaviors, I have to give them all the information they need to make a carefully considered decision. I can't rush them. If they are showing Red (Adventurer) behaviors, they just want to know how fast it goes and "do we have one in Silver!" With practice, the ability to identify a person's predominant behaviors allows him to establish rapport with a customer quickly and communicate the right information.

1) Divide the class into groups of four again. Have each behavioral strength (color) represented as clearly as possible in each group: a strong Planner, Builder, Relater and Adventurer. It may be necessary to take the second or even the third strength (color) to make the foursome, if the group tends to be skewed to certain behaviors.

2) Guess how various characters in ***Harry Potter and the Sorcerer's Stone*** would sort the cards. For example: Harry, Hermione, Ron, Hagrid, Molly Weasley, Professor Dumbledore and Draco Malfoy.
3) Have the teams draw a cartoon with people they know as Planners, Builders, Relaters or Adventurers involved as a team in some activity. Have the colors green, brown, blue or red somewhere on the figure to indicate their strengths.
4) Have each team write and perform a skit with the four characters interacting.
5) Survey the group as to the behavioral strengths of people they have in common, such as teachers, instructors etc. Have them defend their assessment with examples.
6) Have the teams list the behaviors that, for example, a teacher would benefit by bringing up according to whether that person was mainly a Planner, Builder, Relater or Adventurer.
7) Team decides on a physical symbol formed by the group that indicates they have finished an assigned task and that they fulfilled the requirements of the task.
8) Each team creates a song or selects a song that reflects the team's personality.
9) Each team creates a song or selects a song that reflects the Planner, Builder, Relater and Adventurer Part of Self.
10) Each team designs a logo that visually represents the team.
11) Each person, who would like to speak, stands and gives a narrative of his or her "Good-n-New" experience that took place during these activities.
12) Have the teams record their insights on chart paper. Each team reports the results to the group. Post the charts on the wall for all to see.

Wisdom of the Wizards of the World:

Know thyself

Socrates

For the birds that cannot soar, God has provided low branches

Turkish Proverb

Reflection:

1) The Good-n-New for me is ______________________.
2) What excites you most about what you have learned in this lesson?
3) How can you help someone who is having trouble relating with others?
4) List the people in your life and their predominant strength. List the colors or parts of self that are required to communicate successfully with them.

Personal Empowerment Statement:

I now feel strong in being able to bring up that part of me (name the part) for this situation (name situation) or to communicate with (name person).

Friendship

Personal Notes and Reflections

Lesson Two

Friendship

Phase 1 -- Inquire:

Supplies:

1) Chart paper and markers.

Direct the Focus (Objective):

Students discover what they already know and perceive about friendship and relating within a team.

Learning Activities:

The instructor facilitates:

1) Have the students stand in two circles, one inside the other, with half of the group in each circle. The students in each circle face each other. One circle moves clockwise and the other counter clockwise, moving ahead one person at a time. The instructor asks each pair to discuss the following questions or other topics pertinent to the theme for two or three minutes. The statements or questions may be repeated.
    - A) Have each pair share the behaviors that they believe necessary for a solid friendship.
    - B) Have the pairs discuss the pros and cons of belonging to a team.
    - C) Is friendship different between boys and girls than between boys and other boys or girls and other girls?
    - D) Can there be friendship between parents or guardians and young people?
2) Have all participants record "What is Good-n-New" on paper. Assign a couple in the group to tabulate the results on charts. Post the charts on the wall for all to see.

Reflection:

1) The Good-n-New for me is ____.
2) The following youths surprised me _______________. Why? _____________

Personal Empowerment Statement:

I take pride in being a friend to (name the person).

Phase 2 -- Gather:

Supplies:

1) Personality Magic Cards
2) Chart paper and markers
3) ***Harry Potter and the Sorcerer's Stone.***

Direct the Focus (Objective):

Students discover that other people may have different perceptions of what a friend needs to be and what is required to be part of a team.

Learning Activities

Thc instructor facilitates:

Thoughts for Discussion

Our youngest son Matt, is a Relater (Blue). He has always gone out of his way to make friends. At the age of five, he went down our street and knocked on the door of a couple that had just moved into the neighborhood. An older man answered the door and Matt said, "Hi, my name is Matt, what's yours?" The man, taken aback, said" My name is Mr. Finnegan!" Matt said, "Where did you come from, Mr. Finnegan?" Mr. Finnegan said that he had retired in the east and had moved here to retire. Satisfied, Matt said goodbye. The following week, Matt went back to the same house, knocked on the door and when the man again answered, Matt said, "Hi Mr. Finnegan, what is my name?" The man, again taken by surprise, said" I'm sorry, I don't remember your name", to which Matt said," I remembered your name, why don't you remember mine?"

1) Break the group into teams of four. Have each behavioral strength (color) represented as best as possible in each group: a strong Planner, Builder, Relater and Adventurer. It may be necessary to take the second or even the third strength (color) to make the foursome, if the group tends to be skewed to certain behaviors.
2) List and explore the many examples of the instantaneous friendship that occurs in a disaster, such as the result of the terrorist bombing of the Trade Center and Pentagon. Is not the giving of one's life, such as the police, fire fighters and those on the downed plane signify the ultimate in friendship?
3) Read sections of ***Harry Potter and the Sorcerer's Stone*** (Chapter 7) which apply to friendship:
   - A) At first Hermione is a loner and the results were ______________.
   - B) She alienated others by ________________________________.
   - C) How did she become part of the team with Harry and Ron?
   - D) Why is Hagrid a friend to Harry and not Draco Malfoy?
   - E) Does a team have to win to be a strong and successful team?

4) The feelings I experience in reading the Harry Potter books are ____.
5) Have the members decide on an appropriate name for the team.
6) Each person, who would like to speak, stands and gives a narrative of his or her "Good-n-New" experience that took place during these activities.
6) Have the teams record their insights on chart paper. Each team reports the results to the group. Post the charts on the wall for all to see.

Wisdom of the Wizards of the World:

The imaginary friends I had as a kid dropped me,
because all their friends told them I didn't exist.

Aaron Machado

Reflection:

1) The Good-n-New for me is ______________________
2) This is how I respond when I win ______________________
3) This is how I respond when I lose ____________________
4) What happens to your thoughts and feelings when you compete with your friends and win or lose?
5) Is there a connection between your thoughts, feelings and behaviors?

Personal Empowerment Statement:

I take it as a personal challenge to discover the behavioral strengths of anyone with whom I am trying to communicate.

Phase 3 -- Process:

Supplies:

1) Personality Magic Cards
2) Chart paper and markers
3) ***Harry Potter and the Sorcerer's Stone***

Direct the Focus (Objective):

Students determine the basic ingredients for friendship and team building.

Learning Activities

A Story for Discussion

One year, George showed up at the rookie camp to try out for our football team. George was a strong, bright, athletic seventeen year old halfback from a small prairie town who was entering first year Engineering at the University. George was also deaf. How could George hear the plays called in the huddle? How could he respond to the count when the ball was snapped to start the play? How could he take instructions? These problems seemed insurmountable, until his teammates helped develop a system. We used the old "Notre Dame" style huddle, where the other players line up facing the quarterback, so George could read his lips as he called the play. When the signals were called, the fullback simply tapped his hand on his thigh in the same cadence as the count. George went on to be an All Star and later a teacher of hearing-impaired children. Through friendship and teamwork, there was no problem, only different methods.

1) Have the students form the same teams as in the Gather Stage.
2) Is the group you are in acting as a team? What ingredients are missing, if any?
3) The difference between friendship and being a member of a team is ______________________________.
4) How did Harry Potter keep his team together, or were Hermione Granger and Ron Weasley just his friends?
5) Each team member takes a turn adding information or sharing an idea.
6) Two circles are formed with one circle inside the other. One student from each circle faces another student. In these pairs, students discuss the points learned about friendship. Circles rotate two to four times in opposite directions so students discuss questions with new partners.
7) Each person, who would like to speak, stands and gives a narrative of his or her "Good-n-New" experience that took place during these activities.
8) Have the teams record their insights on chart paper. Each team reports the results to the group. Post the charts on the wall for all to see.

Wisdom of the Wizards of the World:

Be a friend to yourself and others will be so too.

Anonymous

There is a magnet in your heart that will attract true friends.
That magnet is unselfishness, thinking of others first...
When you learn to live for others, they will live for you.

Yevgeny Yevtushenko

Reflection:

1) The Good-n-New to Me is ______________________________.
2) Is there a form of friendship in belonging to a successful team?
3) Can a team be successful without a form of friendship?

Personal Empowerment Statement:

I take it as a personal challenge to be a team player on (name the team).

🛠 Phase 4: -- Apply:

Supplies:

1) Personality Magic Cards
2) Chart paper and markers
3) ***Harry Potter and the Sorcerer's Stone***

Direct the Focus (Objective):

Discovery of the major ingredients for any successful team and the crucial elements of friendship.

Learning Activities

The instructor facilitates:

A Tale for Discussion

A little girl was suffering from a rare and serious disease. Her only chance of survival was a blood transfusion. Her little five-year-old brother had developed the antibodies needed to combat the illness. When the doctor asked the little boy if he would be willing to give his blood to save his sister, he hesitated for a moment and said, "Yes, if it will save her."

As the transfusion progressed, the little boy smiled as he could see the color in his sister's cheeks coming back. Then his face grew pale. He asked the doctor: "Will I start to die right away?"

Being young, the little boy misunderstood. He thought that he had to give his sister all of his blood in order to save her. He was prepared to make the ultimate sacrifice when only a lesser one was called for. Understanding and attitude are everything.

1) Form the same teams as in the Inquiry stage. Have them create and perform a skit about a team working together to achieve a goal.
2) Write and perform a friendship song, such as the old song "The more we get together, together, together; the more we get together, the happier we'll be. For your way is my way and my way is your way…".
3) Collect and present a list of songs promoting friendship.
4) Do race and beliefs make it difficult for friendships and teams to exist outside the race or group beliefs?
5) Explore the camaraderie of the French Foreign Legion.
6) Team members brainstorm randomly and rapidly contribute many ideas.
7) Team members create a cheer for the group to be used when the group has accomplished a task and is celebrating.
8) Each person, who would like to speak, stands and gives a narrative of his or her "Good-n-New" experience that took place during these activities.
9) Have the teams record their observations on chart paper and report the results to the whole group. Post the charts on the wall for all to see.

Wisdom of the Wizards of the World:

There is no greater love than this: To lay down one's life for one's friends.

John 15, verse 13

Reflection:

1) The Good-n-New for Me is ______________________________.
2) I treat my friends in the following way ____________________.
3) Do I treat my father, mother, brothers and sisters as friends?
4) I contribute to any team I am on by ______________________.

Personal Empowerment Statement:

I not only want a friend, but I also like being a friend by listening and caring for (Name)

The Spoiled Child

Personal Notes and Reflections

Lesson Three

The Spoiled Child

Phase 1 -- Inquire:

Supplies:

1) Personality Magic Cards
2) Chart paper and markers

Direct the Focus (Objective):

Students distinguish between being "catered-to" in comparison to receiving reasonable gratification.

Learning Activity:

1) Divide the group into teams of four. Have each behavioral strength (color) represented as clearly as possible in each group: a strong Planner, Builder, Relater and Adventurer. It may be necessary to take the second or even the third strength (color) to make the foursome, if the group tends to be skewed to certain behaviors.
2) Share your ideas around the following questions:
   a. What happens when a person's every whim is fulfilled?
   b. Discuss situations where adults spoil children.
   c. Are there spoiled adults or is this limited to children?
3) Each person, who would like to speak, stands and gives a narrative of his or her "Good-n-New" experience that took place during these activities.
4) Have the teams record their observations on chart paper and report the results to the whole group. Post the charts on the wall for all to see.

Reflection:

Ask the Students the following questions:
1. The Good-n-New for me is ______________________________.
2. From the points given, what do you think is the result of being spoiled?
3. A spoiled person communicates by ______________________.
4. I prevent myself from being spoiled by ___________________.

Personal Empowerment Statement:

It is my joy to give and take according to the situation.

☎ Phase 2 - Gather:

Supplies:

1) Personality Magic Cards
2) Chart paper and markers
3) ***Harry Potter and the Sorcerer's Stone***

Direct the Focus (Objective):

Discover the value of discipline and the negative results of catering to every whim.

Learning Activities

The instructor facilitates:

A Tale for Discussion

In high school, one of my classmates was Ron. He had everything. His family was quite well off and Ron was one of the few kids at school who always had a new car. He was also very bright. Often, during the term, Ron would cut classes to pursue other interests but when exam time came around, he showed up and had "crammed" enough to get good marks. Later he went on to become a lawyer. His practice, however, never did very well. He found it very difficult to focus on his client's affairs. You see, Ron always had all his wants fulfilled as a youth and, so unfortunately, he never learned how to want something enough to work hard for it.

1) Form the same teams as in the Inquiry stage.
2) Compare the treatment of Dudley by the Dursleys to their treatment of Harry Potter (Chapters 1 and 2).
3) Compare the treatment of Draco by Lucius Malfoy (Harry, on first meeting Draco, was reminded of Dudley) to Hagrid's treatment of Harry (Chapter 5).
4) What do you think about pouting, sulking and crying when you can't get your way?
5) What is the difference between having one's hand out to receive everything, versus not being able to receive compliments and favors graciously? Refer to Snape's treatment of Harry because Harry's father saved his life. (Chapter 17)
6) Think about how spoiling takes place in a family. Pair with another student to discuss their thoughts, share their thoughts with a larger group or with the class.
7) Each person, who would like to speak, stands and gives a narrative of his or her "Good-n-New" experience that took place during these activities.
8) Have the teams record their observations on chart paper and report the results to the whole group. Post the charts on the wall for all to see.

Wisdom of the Wizards of the World:

The thing that impresses me most about America
is the way parents obey their children

Edward VIII, Duke of Windsor

I know that there are people in this world who do not love their fellow man,
and I hate people like that!

Tom Lehrer

Reflection:

1) The Good-n-New for me is ____.
2) What are positive behaviors when others block desires or goals?

Personal Empowerment Statement:

My strength is in being able to meet challenges (name:) graciously even though blocked by others.

Phase 3 -- Process:

Supplies:

1) Personality Magic Cards
2) Chart paper and markers
3) ***Harry Potter and the Sorcerer's Stone***

Direct the Focus (Objective):

Show how certain behaviors fit into becoming a mature, successful person. Name them and illustrate the behaviors.

Learning Activities

The instructor facilitates:

A Tale for Discussion

Not long ago, I was in the supermarket. While I was waiting in the checkout line, there was an elderly lady in front of me. All of a sudden, a young man, apparently about the age of 11 or 12, walked up and stood in line in front of the lady. He had his arms loaded with soda pop, snacks and junk food. He looked to be wearing about $ 500 worth of the latest and greatest clothing. The lady said. "Excuse me, young man but you are cutting into the line". He said, "I know, but I'm in a hurry. My friends are waiting for me". The lady said, "If I was your mother, I'd teach you to have respect for other people's rights." He retorted, "If you were my mother, I'd commit suicide!" To which the lady said, "If I was your mother, I'd do it for you!"

1) Form the same teams as in the Gather stage.

2) Read or listen to pertinent passages from the Dursley's spoiling of Dudley and the treatment of Draco Malfoy by his father Lucius.
3) Create a Harry Potter web site focusing on how to build positive character behaviors for successful communication.
4) Create a song, rap or poem contrasting between a spoiled and a well-adjusted person.
5) Is always talking and never listening a form of being spoiled?
6) How do one's peers react to a spoiled person in a group?
7) Each person, who would like to speak, stands and gives a narrative of his or her "Good-n-New" experience that took place during these activities.
8) Have the teams record their observations on chart paper and report the results to the whole group. Post the charts on the wall for all to see.

The Wisdom of the Wizards of the World:

Be charitable and indulgent to everyone but thyself.

Joseph Joubert

Reflection:

1) The Good-n-New for me is ________________________________.
2) I must take the following steps in order to develop a more likeable personality ____.
3) It is important to me to have friends, because ____________________.

Personal Empowerment Statements:

I enjoy sharing and giving recognition to (name______)

Phase 4: - Apply:

Supplies:

1) Personality Magic Cards
2) Chart paper and markers
3) ***Harry Potter and the Sorcerer's Stone***

Direct the Focus (Objective):

Identify the behaviors for successful teams and friendship.

Learning Activities

The instructor facilitates:

A Tale for Discussion

The game of football is a good representation of people achieving success by working together. There are eleven men on the field and each has a role to play. While the quarterback, running backs and receivers are the ones who get all the press, their success is totally dependent on every other player performing his assigned tasks well. Critical to a smooth functioning team, is an appreciation by each player that every teammate has an important contribution to make. A missed block by a lineman can turn a touchdown play into an incomplete pass or a loss of yardage. Like a quality watch, every wheel has to turn as it should or the time is wrong. The ball-hog (spoiled child) or glory seeker destroys the team.

1) Form the same teams as in the Inquiry stage.
2) Create posters for the classroom and for the students to take home.
3) Give each person a balloon and have him or her put her or his name on it. Play suitable music in the background. The rule is that if they either break their own balloon or another's they are out of the game. Have the game begin with them bouncing the balloons in the air. Then, as in life, let the balloon drop and note how it bounces back. Then have them pass their balloons amongst each other.
4) Note how Harry had the joy of sharing his good fortune for the first time with Ron Weasley on the train.
5) Each person, who would like to speak, stands and gives a narrative of his or her "Good-n-New" experience that took place during these activities.
6) Have the teams record their observations on chart paper and report the results to the whole group. Post the charts on the wall for all to see.

The Wisdom of the Wizards of the World:

What's done to children, they will do to society

Karl Menninger

Reflection:

1) The Good-n-New for me is ______________________________.
2) The behaviors I consider crucial for being part of a team are ____________.
3) The following are some of the vocabulary words used by the likeable personality ______________________________.

Personal Empowerment Statement:

One powerful behavior I have is my capacity to share, especially with those less fortunate than myself.

CAPTAIN COURAGEOUS
C
C
Mark Bezenar

Personal Notes and Reflections

Lesson Four

Captain Courageous

Phase 1 -- Inquire:

Supplies:

a. Personality Magic Cards
b. Chart paper and markers

Direct the Focus (Objective):

The students identify various forms of physical and mental courage that they recognize in themselves.

Learning Activity

The instructor facilitates:

1) Break the class into groups of four. Have each behavioral strength (color) represented as clearly as possible in each group: a strong Planner, Builder, Relater and Adventurer. It may be necessary to take the second or even the third strength (color) to make the foursome, if the group tends to be skewed to certain behaviors.
2) On the chart paper, list two column headings: Physical and Mental. Have the students cite at least five or six examples of each type of courage and record them on the paper. Why is each example courageous? Are there degrees of courage? Record the answers on the chart paper.
3) Is there a difference between courage and daring? The following are examples ____.
4) Each person, who would like to speak, stands and gives a narrative of his or her "Good-n-New" experience that took place during these activities.
5) Have the teams record their observations on chart paper and report the results to the whole group. Post the charts on the wall for all to see.

Reflection:

1) The Good-n-New for me is ________________________________.
2) Some courageous acts that I have done in my life are ________________.
3) I develop courageous behaviors by ____________________________.

Personal Empowerment Statement:

I take great pride in being able to stand up for my beliefs. At the same time, I am open to new information, which may adjust my beliefs.

Phase 2 -- Gather:

Supplies:

1) Chart paper and markers
2) Personality Magic Cards
3) ***Harry Potter and the Sorcerer's Stone***

Direct the Focus (Objective):

Students discover the differences between what they think courage involves and aspects of courage in the real world.

Learning Activity

The instructor facilitates:

A Story for Discussion

Our daughter loves to sing. She had begun singing at the age of five, at the urging of our oldest son, who was then a professional musician in a rock band. At times she could be persuaded to sing at family gatherings, but she was quite self-conscious about doing so. When she was eleven, her Grandfather passed away and her Grandmother asked her to sing three hymns at the funeral with only a few days to prepare.

As the day of the funeral approached, she said she was ready, but she developed a nervous sigh, indicating that she was holding in her fear. At the funeral, about five minutes before she was to perform the first hymn, she became sick to her stomach and almost fainted. We were confident that she would do a very good job and reassured her. She then walked up to the microphone and sang beautifully. Now twenty-five, with a professional singing career, she has never been nervous before a performance since.

1) Have the students form the same teams as in the Inquiry stage.
2) Have them pick out passages, which illustrate courage in ***Harry Potter and the Sorcerers Stone,*** such as in chapters 9 and 16.
3) What were you thinking during this activity?
4) List the different examples of physical and intellectual courage. A physical example would be Hermione going over to distract Snape, who she thought was responsible for making Harry's broomstick uncontrollable, in Chapter 11.
5) Refer to the musical stage play and film *Oliver,* where Fagan sings the song with the lyrics: "I'm reviewing the situation!" This is a necessary strategy in certain situations. Harry and Ron changed strategies because of the interference of Neville, Hermione and Peeves (Chapter 9). Indicate the outcome and give the reasons why.
6) Teams prepare a performance or presentation based on a synthesis of what they learned in this lesson.

7) Each person, who would like to speak, stands and gives a narrative of his or her "Good-n-New" experience that took place during these activities.
8) Have the teams record their observations on chart paper and report the results to the whole group. Post the charts on the wall for all to see.

The Wisdom of the Wizards of the World:

Courage is rightly esteemed as the first of human qualities,
because it is the quality which guarantees all the others.

Winston Churchill

Reflection:

1) The Good-n-New for me is ______________________________.
2) The following situations at home call for me to take a stand

____.

3) The following situations at school call for me to take a stand

____.

Personal Empowerment Statement:

I have the courage to build a strong mind as well as a strong body.

Phase 3 -- Process:

Supplies:

1) Personality Magic Cards
2) Chart paper and markers
3) ***Harry Potter and the Sorcerer's Stone***

Direct the Focus (Objective):

Students realize that the virtues of all four of the Hogwarts houses are crucial for being courageous.

Learning Activities

The instructor facilitates:

A Story for Discussion

Skiing was the winter sport for our family. Introducing our five children to the ski hill was a harrowing experience, as we could only pay attention to one at a time. When each child's lesson was over we showed him/her the small bunny hill. My husband and I instructed them to play on the hill but under no circumstances were they to try the towrope. "Just stay and play on the small hill until we come to get you!"

At lunchtime, we gathered to have a bite to eat. We were missing a child! We looked up the hill and schussing down the hill in a little red suit was our 6 year old. After calming down, we asked him why would he disobey us and do such a

dangerous thing. Although not appreciated then, his courageous little answer was: "It just looked like so much fun that I had to try it!"
Giants of courage like Amelia Earhart, early aviatrix, who challenged conventional limits by attempting to fly solo around the world; to Chuck Yeager, the test pilot who extended the limits of manned flight; to Jacques Cousteau, scientist and oceanographer, whose daring undersea explorations expanded our understanding of the depths of the oceans; to our friend Harry Potter; who just had to try it!

1) Have the students form teams in accordance with the four houses of Hogwarts. (Chapter 7)

   Gryffindor (brave and daring) **Hufflepuff** (loyal and hardworking)
   Slytherin (cunning and sly) **Ravenclaw** (wise and witty, mascot is an eagle)

2) Have each team write out and draw a poster to attract others to join their house.
3) Set up a debate between the houses. Each group defends its house's behaviors as the most important for being courageous in situations.
4) What changes in awareness occurred from the activity?
5) Have the teams create a song or select a song that reflects the four houses.
6) Each person, who would like to speak, stands and gives a narrative of his or her "Good-n-New" experience that took place during these activities.
7) Have the teams record their observations on chart paper and report the results to the whole group. Post the charts on the wall for all to see.

The Wisdom of the Wizards of the World:

The courage we desire and prize is not the courage to die decently, but to live manfully.

Thomas Carlyle

Reflection:

1) The Good-n-New for me is ____.
2) Are the behaviors of all four houses necessary for being courageous? _______
3) I learned from the following from others ______________________________
   ____.
4) I need the behaviors of all four houses to communicate and succeed in life for the following reasons ____.

Personal Empowerment Statement:

I am proud of being able to be decisive, (Builder Part of Me) daring, (Adventurer Part of Me), loyal (Relater Part of Me) and wise (Planner Part of Me) according to the situation.

Phase 4: -- Apply:

Supplies:

1) Personality Magic Cards
2) Chart paper and markers
3) ***Harry Potter and the Sorcerer's Stone***

Direct the Focus (Objective):

Students identify courageous behaviors and situations pertinent to them.

Learning Activities

The instructor facilitates:

A Story for Discussion

Very early one morning (1:00 A. M.) my 9-year-old son came into the bedroom sobbing. I asked him: "What's wrong?" He explained: "A couple of weeks ago, I stole a chocolate bar at the local drug store." The incident had played on his mind and he hadn't been able to sleep since. After discussing the situation, my child and I decided that the best thing to do was to go back to the Drug Store and make amends. The proprietor of the store thanked him very much for being so brave and courageous.

1) Have the same teams as in the Inquiry stage.
2) Choose selections from ***Harry Potter and the Sorcerer's Stone*** that indicate the value of Harry having both the characteristics of a Slytherin and a Gryffindor and how this saved his life.
3) Explore key characteristics that an employer would look for in an employee.
4) What behaviors are necessary for team spirit?
5) What characteristics would be valuable for success after leaving home?
6) In what ways are you a different person from the person who began this lesson?
7) Each team member takes a turn adding information or sharing an idea: each class member shares an insight or a new learning.
8) Each person, who would like to speak, stands and gives a narrative of his or her "Good-n-New" experience that took place during these activities.
9) Have the teams record their observations on chart paper and report the results to the whole group. Post the charts on the wall for all to see.

Wisdom of the Wizards of the World:

The paradox of courage is that a man must be a little careless of his life even in order to keep it.

G. K. Chesterton

Reflection:

1) The Good-n-New for me is ________________________________.
2) Occasions present to me now that illustrate strength of character are ____.

Personal Empowerment Statement:

I feel a sense of terrific strength when I stand up for what I believe, that is ____!

FALSE JUDGEMENT

Personal Notes and Reflections

Lesson Five

False Judgments

Phase 1 -- Inquire:

Supplies:

1) Personality Magic Cards
2) Chart paper and markers

Direct the Focus (Objective):

Students discover that sometimes their observations, and many times their first impressions of people, may be completely mistaken.

Learning Activities

The instructor facilitates:

1) Break the students into groups of four. Have each behavioral strength (color) represented as clearly as possible in each group: a strong Planner, Builder, Relater and Adventurer. It may be necessary to take the second or even the third strength (color) to make the foursome, if the group tends to be skewed to certain behaviors.
2) Have the students give examples of times they have experienced having the blame put on someone, or themselves, when innocent.
3) How can gossip destroy innocent people?
4) What does the word bias mean?
5) When have we acted with prejudice?
6) Do those with strong Relater behaviors have a tendency to talk about people?
7) Indicate five insights realized about accusing innocent people in this lesson.
8) Each person, who would like to speak, stands and gives a narrative of his or her "Good-n-New" experience that took place during these activities.
9) Have the teams record their observations on chart paper and report the results to the whole group. Post the charts on the wall for all to see.

Reflection:

1) The Good-n-New for me is____.
2) Are there persons about whom I have received misguided information that I found out later to be untrue? ____.
3) If I gossip, I do the following damage ______________________________.
4) List a time or times when your first impression changed later_____________.

Personal Empowerment Statement:

I take pride in assuming a person is innocent until absolutely proven guilty.

Phase 2 -- Gather:

Supplies:

1) Personality Magic Cards
2) Chart paper and markers
3) ***Harry Potter and the Sorcerer's Stone***.

Direct the Focus (Objective):

The value of assuming innocence until guilt is proven.

Learning Activities

The instructor facilitates:

A Story for Discussion

One of my children was accused of plagiarism. This is a child who was a very avid reader and had excellent comprehension. His previous teachers had told us that his vocabulary was far above the average child of his age. Explaining this to his teacher was all for naught. He stated: "No eleven year old can possibly write an essay of this quality!" Today this "little gifted" child is a successful businessperson, musician and writer.
A newspaper editor fired Walt Disney because he "lacked imagination and had no good ideas"
What damage may be done when adults do not recognize the creativity of others?

1) Put the students in a line. Start by giving the following message in writing to the first student: "John and Mary were out last night riding their bicycles and John was hit by a speeding car!" Each student whispers the message to the next student in line. Have the last student report to the group the final message heard.
2) Break into the same teams as the Inquiry phase
3) What new insights have you gained from the whispering of a message from one to another, as above?
4) Refer to passages in ***Harry Potter and the Sorcerer's Stone*** regarding Snape. Discuss how and why Harry, Hermione and Ron misjudged him.
5) Have the students form mixed color groups according to how they sorted the cards (Planner, Builder, Relater and Adventurer strengths in each). Have them consider the following:
   a) Are there times when keeping a secret is not binding?
   b) Explore the accusations and miscarriage of justice in regard to Hagrid.
   b) Have the students cite films or TV shows with a theme of miscarriage of justice.
6) Are there occasions when it is opportune to explain the circumstances and at other times not explain them? An example would be when Dumbledore

explained to Harry why Snape acts as he does; yet Dumbledore did not reveal all of Harry's past to him. (Chapter 17)

7) What have you learned that you didn't know before?
8) Each person, who would like to speak, stands and gives a narrative of his or her "Good-n-New" experience that took place during these activities.
9) Have the teams record their observations on chart paper and report the results to the whole group. Post the charts on the wall for all to see.

Wisdom of the Wizards of the World:

Superstition, bigotry and prejudice, ghosts though they are, cling tenaciously to life: they are shades armed with tooth and claw. They must be grappled with unceasingly, for it is a fateful part of human destiny that it is condemned to wage perpetual war against ghosts.

Victor Hugo from *Les Miserable*

Reflection:

1) The Good-n-New for me is ______________________________.
2) The persons or situations I may have misjudged are ________________.
3) State why it is important to keep a personal secret someone has confided to you.

Personal Empowerment Statement:

I enjoy having the strength to listen to someone's challenges and not reveal them, unless their problems could hurt or destroy the person, or others, emotionally or physically.

Phase 3 -- Process:

Supplies:

1) Personality Magic Cards
2) Chart paper and markers
3) ***Harry Potter and the Sorcerer's Stone*** and other texts from the Harry Potter Series as reference.

Direct the Focus (Objective):

Students learn to apply the maxim: *"Innocent until proven guilty."* Even then, leave room for human error.

Learning Activities

The instructor facilitates:

A Story for Discussion

Bobby was a classmate of one of our sons in High School. His parents had moved away to another City and Bobby stayed on to complete the school year. He lived in an apartment with his brother. One night, a teenager, wearing a balaclava, jeans and a T-shirt, robbed a local gas station. The attendant who was robbed told the Police that he was positive that the robber was Bobby. " I'm sure it was him, he was the same size and his voice and movements were the same. I've known him for years!" Bobby was arrested and charged with the crime. He denied committing the crime, but couldn't prove it. While the investigation continued, Bobby's classmates discussed how dumb Bobby was to have robbed someone who would recognize him so easily! About two weeks later, the real robber was discovered and, sure enough, he was the same size and sounded " a bit" like Bobby. His friends and classmates had let him down.

1) Set up a Court, as in real life. Have the defense take Hagrid or Snape. The defense and prosecution may only take the evidence from the 1st book. Another trial could be held later, allowing evidence from the other texts of the Harry Potter Series. Compare the decisions.
2) Set up a skit, with a court set up as in real life. Role-play a defendant, with false evidence given and later discovered.
3) Each person, who would like to speak, stands and gives a narrative of his or her "Good-n-New" experience that took place during these activities.
4) Have the teams record their observations on chart paper and report the results to the whole group. Post the charts on the wall for all to see.

Wisdom of the Wizards of the World:

Calumny requires no proof. The throwing out of malicious imputations against any character leaves a stain, which no after-refutation can wipe out. To create an unfavorable impression, it is not necessary that certain things should be true, but that they have been said

William Hazlitt

Reflection:

1) The Good-n-New for me is____.
2) In the trial held above, what was the main behavioral strength of the defendant, prosecutor, judge, witnesses and jury? ____________________
3) How did this influence their presentation? _________________________

Personal Empowerment Statement:

I take pride in waiting until all the evidence is in before making any judgments and even then allow new evidence to come in that may change my viewpoint.

Phase 4: -- Apply:

Supplies:

1) Personality Magic Cards
2) Chart paper and markers
3) ***Harry Potter and the Sorcerer's Stone***

Direct the Focus (Objective):

The Students learn how to safeguard the accuracy of their judgments in the best way possible, through an active feedback strategy.

Learning Activities:

A Story for Discussion

One of the best ways of being objective is to develop active listening skills. There were a number of student mentors who became very proficient in ways of understanding others. Monty, 20 years old and one of the mentors, was very quiet and unassuming. He had the art of giving excellent, understanding feedback facilitation. As fate would have it, he was involved in a tragic auto accident that took his life. Although he had left high school a couple of years before, the church was packed with young people. Dozens of conversations centered on how Monty's empathetic understanding had saved their lives from tragedy. As the song goes, "only the good die young."

1) A Feedback Activity: Divide the students into pairs. To the degree possible, have each pair made up of the different behavioral strengths (**not** two Planners, Builders, Relaters or Adventurers). Each twosome should stand at an angle, not facing each other. One is designated as the speaker, the other the listener.
   a. The speaker has 3 minutes to talk about something that is important to her or him.
   b. The listener IS ONLY ALLOWED TO GIVE A FEEDBACK SUMMARY. For example, if the speaker talks about an exciting holiday, the listener may respond "You had a great time on your vacation!"
   c. Never, ever add personal experiences or opinions, such as: "You know I had a terrific time on my vacation, too!" Do not ask probing questions, such as "What did you do on your vacation?" This is not the object of the exercise unless the speaker chooses to share the experience.
   d. Listening is a very challenging exercise. Few people are capable of listening to the world of ideas and feelings of another. Most people have to stick in their two cents worth. Such expressions as "You know when I was your age" or "I know how you feel!" are taboo if you want to understand and enter the world of another. **The speaker cares little of what you did at that age or how you feel!** This is a clever trick the listener uses to flip roles and get the speaker to listen to her or him.
   e. The ability to listen properly is so poor that many feel they have to pay someone to listen to their problems and concerns. This is called "paid friendship" and is seldom productive.
2) What feelings did you experience during your listening session?
3) Cite and examine the accusations of Dudley Dursley, Uncle Vernon and Aunt Petunia in regard to Harry. Describe how you would feel if you were Harry.

4) What excites you most about what you have learned today?
5) What do you want to do differently in your life as a result of your new understandings?
6) Out of all the information you talked about today, what do you think are the most crucial points for you to remember? Why?
7) Each person, who would like to speak, stands and gives a narrative of his or her "Good-n-New" experience that took place during these activities.
8) Have the teams record their observations on chart paper and report the results to the whole group. Post the charts on the wall for all to see.

Wisdom of the Wizards of the World:

Seek not to know who said this or that, but take note of what has been said

Thomas Kempis

Reflection:

1) The Good-n-new for me is ______________________________________.
2) Is the Relater Part of Me so strong that I seldom hear anything but my own voice? ____
____
3) When I choose, I take pride in listening and doing my best to understand a person's feelings and ideas______________________________________.

Personal Empowerment Statement:

I take great pride in being able to keep my mouth shut and ears open in order to listen objectively to a person's (name) feelings and ideas, when I choose.

Child Abuse and Bullies

Personal Notes and Reflections

Lesson Six

Child Abuse and Bullies

Phase 1 -- Inquire:

Instructor or Parent: This chapter must be handled very delicately, as some of the students may presently be experiencing abuse by adults or other youths.

Direct the Focus (Objective):

Students describe what they know about bullies and abuse by adults and other youths. They distinguish between physical and mental abuse

Supplies:

1) Personality Magic Cards
2) Chart paper and markers

Learning Activity:

The instructor facilitates:

1) Break the students into groups of four. Have each behavioral strength (color) represented as clearly as possible in each group: a strong Planner, Builder, Relater and Adventurer. It may be necessary to take the second or even the third strength (color) to make the foursome, if the group tends to be skewed to certain behaviors.
2) Have the members of each group describe instances in their lives when they have either faced bullies, suffered abuse from adults or seen it happen to others.
3) Have them put two columns on the chart paper with the headings, "physical abuse" and "verbal abuse". List examples of each.
4) Does one type cause more damage than the other?
5) What were you thinking about during this activity?
6) What new insights did you gain in this activity?
7) Each person, who would like to speak, stands and gives a narrative of his or her "Good-n-New" experience that took place during these activities.
8) Have the teams record their observations on chart paper and report the results to the whole group. Post the charts on the wall for all to see.

Reflection:

1) The Good-n-New for me is ______________________________________.
2) The difference between discipline and abuse is __________________________.
3) The way I handle a bully now is __________________________________.

Personal Empowerment Statement:

I treat people the way I would like to be treated.

Phase 2 -- Gather:

Supplies:

1) Chart paper and markers
2) Personality Magic Cards
3) ***Harry Potter and the Sorcerer's Stone***

Direct the Focus (Objective):

Have the students compare their present knowledge with new information supplied from Harry Potter, this text and examples from the instructor or parent.

Learning Activities

The instructor facilitates:

A Story for Discussion:

When I was a youth counselor in the high school system, a principal sent me a young boy who constantly had bruises and cuts. On talking to the youth, he explained that the only way he was allowed to be with a group of boys was to allow them to beat him up. This was the price he had to pay to belong to the group.

1) Have the students regroup in the same teams as in the Inquire phase above.
2) Have them read passages from ***Harry Potter and the Sorcerer's Stone*** such as Harry being forced to live under the stairs by the Dursleys. (Chapter 2)
3) Have the members of the groups discuss the behaviors of Draco Malfoy's sidekicks at Hogwarts, Crabbe and Goyle (Chapter 9).
4) Compare Draco's gang (Chapter 6) to the behaviors of Dudley's gang (Chapter 2).
5) What does it mean to be a coward?
6) What do you think of the saying "the survival of the fittest?"
7) Make two columns. Place "pro" above one and "con" above the other. List the pros and cons of belonging to a gang or group.

8) What are some options for both being able to belong to a group, and retaining dignity?
9) What is the difference between a football or basketball team and a gang? Or is there?
10) What new insights did you gain from these activities?
11) What were you thinking during these activities?
12) What were you feeling during these activities?
13) Each person, who would like to speak, stands and gives a narrative of his or her "Good-n-New" experience that took place during these activities.
14) Have the teams record their observations on chart paper and report the results to the whole group. Post the charts on the wall for all to see.

Wisdom of the Wizards of the World:

Character is what you are in the dark.

Dwight L. Moody

Cowards die many times before their deaths;
The valiant never taste of death but once.

Shakespeare, *Julius Caesar*

Reflection:

1) The Good-n-New for me is ______________________________.
2) Have the youths compare the instances in ***Harry Potter and the Sorcerers Stone*** to their own experiences. How do they compare?
3) The costs for me to join a club, group or gang are ____________________.
4) The advantages for me to belong to a club, group or gang are ___________.

Personal Empowerment Statement:

I am open to new information that will help me understand both people (name the person) and situations (name the situation).

Phase 3 -- Process:

Supplies:

1) Personality Magic Cards
2) Chart paper and markers
3) ***Harry Potter and the Sorcerer's Stone***

Direct the Focus (Objective):

Have the students experience a team effort rather than a gang mentality.

Learning Activity:

The instructor facilitates:

A Story for Discussion

Sometimes even true information, shared in confidence and gossiped to others, may cause untold damage. A young lady was in the hospital with a nervous breakdown. She had been going through the traumatic experience of her parents going through a divorce. She confided and shared her confused feelings with someone whom she thought was a friend. This "friend" gossiped and spread her private feelings throughout the school. The students began to tease and embarrass her about the divorce and their taunting ended in her hospitalization. Give any example you have experienced.

1) Have the students regroup as they did in the Inquiry phase. Have them demonstrate and show the difference between negative put downs and positive put ups. Have a skit contrasting the two.
2) Have the teams point out possible ways of stopping abuse, or surviving in instances of physical and mental abuse they have seen. (Care needs to be taken at this point, as some members might be subject to abuse presently.)
3) Of all the material you have discussed in this lesson, what do you think are the most crucial points for you to remember? Why?
4) Each person, who would like to speak, stands and gives a narrative of his or her "Good-n-New" experience that took place during these activities.
5) Have the teams record their observations on chart paper and report the results to the whole group. Post the charts on the wall for all to see.

Wisdom of the Wizards of the World:

To bring up a child in the way he or she should go,
travel that way yourself once in a while.

Josh Billings

Reflection:

1. The Good-n-New for me is ________________________________.
2. What have I found out about bullying and abuse?
3. This is important to me because ____________________________.
4. What is the difference between a gang and a team? May a football or basketball team actually be a gang?

Personal Empowerment Statement:

I find it fulfilling to keep private, personal information confidential.

🛠 Phase 4: -- Apply:

Supplies:

1) Personality Magic Cards
2) Chart paper and markers

Direct Focus (Objective):

The students demonstrate the value of a team working together.

Learning Activities

The instructor facilitates:

A Story for Discussion

Not too many stories with happy endings came out from the Holocaust, during World War II. But I heard of a wonderful story of two young children about 12 years old. A little boy was in a concentration camp, confused, lonely and wondering what it was all about. As he approached the barbed wire fence surrounding the camp, he saw a young girl on the outside of the fence looking in. No words were exchanged. She was able to hand him an apple through the barbed wires. They continued these meetings for a number of days, until he told her not to come back, as he was being transferred to another camp. Years went by and the young man eventually ended up in New York City. One day, he reluctantly accepted a blind date through a friend of his. While conversing, they discovered that she was the little girl who had brought him the apple every day. Needless to say, they married and have celebrated more than fifty years of marriage.

1) Have the students regroup as they did in the Inquiry phase. Have them draw up a strategy for preventing abuse.
2) Have them draw up charts, posters, cartoons and slogans of respect for others. Post them where others may see them.
3) Have the learners list possible abuse situations presently in THEIR world.
4) List possible strategies to alleviate the situations.
5) Create and write skits illustrating the above.
6) Write or perform a song (lyrics and music) about having good relationships with others.
7) Write and perform a TV commercial about respect for others and the power of group friendships or family ties.
8) What do you want to do differently in your life as a result of your new understandings?
9) Each person, who would like to speak, stands and gives a narrative of his or her "Good-n-New" experience that took place during these activities.
10) Have the teams record their observations on chart paper and report the results to the whole group. Post the charts on the wall for all to see.

Wisdom of the Wizards of the World:

Roming in thought over the Universe, I saw the little that is Good steadily hastening towards immortality
And the vast of all that is call'd Evil I saw hastening to merge itself and become lost and dead.

Walt Whitman, *Roming in Thought*

All cruelty springs from weakness

Seneca

Reflection:

1) The Good-n-New for me is ______________________________.
2) I apply the following to my life ______________________________.

Personal Empowerment Statement:

I have a sense of power and triumph in appreciating and relating positively with (name of a person difficult to relate with in the past).

The Adventurer

Personal Notes and Reflections

Lesson Seven

The Adventurer

Phase 1 -- Inquire:

Supplies:

1) Personality Magic Cards
2) Chart paper and markers

Direct the Focus (Objective):

Students learn the value of good humor and fun in life.

Learning Activities

The instructor facilitates:

1) Break the students into groups of four. Have each behavioral strength (color) represented as clearly as possible in each group: a strong Planner, Builder, Relater and Adventurer. It may be necessary to take the second or even the third strength (color) to make the foursome, if the group tends to be skewed to certain behaviors.
2) Have them list what they consider adventurous and courageous. Is there a difference?
3) In the adventurer part of self, describe at least seven fun filled and exciting aspects.
4) What about using a person's race and/or handicaps to get a laugh? Describe and indicate examples.
5) Is there a tendency for the Adventurer part of Self to USE persons as the butt of his or her joke?
6) Each person, who would like to speak, stands and gives a narrative of his or her "Good-n-New" experience that took place during these activities.
7) Have the teams record their observations on chart paper and report the results to the whole group. Post the charts on the wall for all to see.

Reflection:

1) The Good-n-New for me is ________________________________.
2) What were the differences between what persons with different behaviors found exciting and challenging? This surprised me because _____________.

Personal Empowerment Statement:

I am exhilarated when I discover new opportunities.

Phase 2 -- Gather:

Supplies:

1) Personality Magic Cards
2) Chart paper and markers
3) ***Harry Potter and the Sorcerer's Stone***

Direct the Focus (Objective):

The students distinguish between being adventurous and being reckless. Have them note that what may be considered an adventure by one, may not be considered so by another.

Learning Activities

The instructor facilitates:

A Story for Discussion

My childhood was spent as an only child on a prairie farm. We were snowed in for two or three months, with temperatures 30 to 50 below. As I always say in my seminars, "I was so frightened of people, I could not lead a group in silent prayer!" It was a challenge for me when we moved to the city and definitely out of my comfort zone. When at University, I took one of the most courageous actions of my life. I joined the University Acting club that met at the end of the year in competition with other Universities. I remember the competition well - fifty years later. Prestigious judges of the arts and critics from the major newspapers attended.

It was even more of a challenge, as we chose one of the earliest plays ever written in English: ***"The Second Shepherds Play."*** I only remember my knees shaking, as I was one of the shepherds. I also remember how the judges congratulated me and the cast for our bravery in choosing such a difficult presentation. All the other universities chose easy, modern plays. We got excellent reviews for our acting. We lost first place only because of our background scenery. The judges commented: "Your set design was to be the middle ages. Your stage set could have a few siding boards put on the 2x4s and it would have passed for a 20th century condo!"

1) Have the students form the same teams as in the Inquiry stage.
2) What happens to your actions or your skills after reading Harry Potter books?
3) What adventurous behaviors do you exhibit after reading Harry Potter books?
4) What is the difference between adventurous and reckless? Have the teams indicate what would be an adventure for them.

5) Have the members of the group indicate what they consider adventurous. Is it true that what seems adventurous to one person may not be adventurous to another? Prove.
6) Have the groups create an adventure skit, posters, or even the lyrics of a song like "Foot Loose."
7) Show how an entrepreneur, creative person or sales person must have strong adventurer behaviors. *"Go where no man has ever gone before."* List some of the contributions of Adventurers to the making of our civilization, such as the pioneers, astronauts or the military during World War Two or Viet Nam.
8) Discuss and list the Adventure Part of Self as it applies to the life of ***Harry Potter.*** In what way is your life comparable to Harry's adventures in his discovery of knowledge, physical challenges and taking chances to save his friends?
9) Explore the negative humor Draco Malfoy directed at Harry and Ron compared with that of George and Fred Wesley. Make two headings on the chart paper, one for each of Draco and the Weasleys, with a list under each.
10) Discuss the adventurer part of Neville Longbottom who, in spite of the danger, went out to warn and help Harry, Ron and Hermione.
11) What do you want to do differently in your life as a result of your new understandings?
12) Each person, who would like to speak, stands and gives a narrative of his or her "Good-n-New" experience that took place during these activities.
13) Have the teams record their observations on chart paper and report the results to the whole group. Post the charts on the wall for all to see.

Wisdom of the Wizards of the World:

A man's reach should exceed his grasp, or what's a heaven for?

Alfred Lord Tennyson

Reflection:

1) The Good-n-New for me is ____________________________________.
2) My experience in this class was ________________________________.

Personal Empowerment Statement:

I have the courage and strength to take calculated risks, which lead me to success.

Phase 3 -- Process:

Supplies:

1) Personality Magic Cards
2) Chart paper and markers
3) ***Harry Potter and the Sorcerer's Stone***

Direct the Focus (Objective):

The students learn to develop and reinforce the Adventurer Part of Self.

Learning Activities

The instructor facilitates:

A Story for Discussion

A close friend of mine has a very adventure-oriented son. He knew from being familiar with Personality Magic, that to hinder his spirited son would be a disaster. Although having a strong Builder orientation, he appreciated his son's behavioral orientation. He allowed him to join clubs active in climbing and other physically challenging activities. As a result, his son learned safety precautions and shared his whereabouts with his parents. If the father had acted as many parents do, his son would be out on the streets spinning wheels and taking uncalculated risks. The reward for his parents was that one of his first jobs was on a cruise ship and he even went climbing up to one of the lower camps of Mount Everest.
They just recently went out on a fishing trip in the mountains and came back with no fish, but a fun time was had.

1) Have the students form the same teams as the Inquiry stage.
2) Have them present an adventure story skit, complete with posters.
3) Have them gather jokes, cartoons or funny stories. Ask the group for volunteers who will collect positive growth jokes and cartoons and post one each day. Have those with an artistic flare create their own cartoons and posters.
4) What do you think of those who make a joke out of someone else's weakness, social status or race? Refer to Draco Malfoy's constant belittling of Harry and his references to the poverty of Ron Weasley.
5) Collect instances of the tricks and jokes of Ron and Fred. What is your evaluation of them?
6) What excites you most about what you learned in this lesson?
7) Each person, who would like to speak, stands and gives a narrative of his or her "Good-n-New" experience that took place during these activities.
8) Have the teams record their observations on chart paper and report the results to the whole group. Post the charts on the wall for all to see.

Wisdom of the Wizards of the World:

If Only Life Were This Easy:

* If you messed up your life, you could press "Ctrl, Alt, Delete" and start all over!
* To get your daily exercise, just click on "run", if you needed a break from life, click on suspend.
* Hit "any key" to continue life when ready.
* To add/remove someone in your life, click settings and control panel.
* To improve your appearance, just adjust the display settings.
* When you lose your car keys, click on find.
* "Help" with the chores is just a click away.
* Auto insurance wouldn't be necessary. You would use your diskette to recover from a crash.
* And, we could click on "SEND NOW" and a Pizza would be on its way!

Net Dummy Humor

Reflection:

1) The Good-n-New for me is ______________________________.
2) Do I smile often?

Personal Empowerment Statement:

I make certain I have at least one laugh movement every day.

Phase 4: -- Apply:

Supplies:

1) Personality Magic Cards
2) Chart paper and markers
3) ***Harry Potter and the Sorcerer's Stone***

Direct Focus (Objective):

The students create their own list of what is courageous for them.

Learning Activities

The instructor facilitates:

A Story for Discussion

My 18-year-old son, with only a couple of weeks left to becoming a full-fledged soldier, was involved in a terrible accident. It led to him being discharged. As a true Adventurer, this was not to hold him back. After taking some time to heal, he left for Europe, telling us that he was going to a Club Med as a Scuba Diving instructor. In fact, his intention was to join the French Foreign Legion. After a week or two, he realized he would have to renounce his country and his name to join the Legion and he was not prepared to do that. When we asked him why he had done it, he said that he had not finished his training and it was something he felt he had to do. Reason prevailed, however and he went to the Caribbean as a Scuba Instructor and now runs two companies there.

1) Have the students form the same teams as in the Inquiry stage.
2) Have them present, as teams, challenges that are available. For example, do some bullies need to be stopped, are some peers the butt of misplaced humor?
3) List possible safe local places for excitement and challenge, such as Scuba Diving schools, acting and outdoor clubs, "Outward Bound" or mountain climbing training.
4) Make a poster and write a "joke of the day" for the classroom.
5) Would you like to join the French Foreign Legion or the Navy Seals? Why?
6) Where may you be able to apply what you have learned in this lesson outside this classroom?
7) Each person, who would like to speak, stands and gives a narrative of his or her "Good-n-New" experience that took place during these activities.
8) Have the teams record their observations on chart paper and report the results to the whole group. Post the charts on the wall for all to see.

Wisdom of the Wizards of the World:

Have a howl movement every day!

Dr. Laurence Martel, Intellearn

It's terrible to run out of mountains to climb.

Guy Vander Jagt

Reflection:

1) The Good-n-New for me is ________________________________.
2) This is my courageous behavioral list ________________________.
3) I dare to be great by ____________________________________

Personal Empowerment Statement:

I dare to be great, mentally and physically, according to the situation.

Authority Rides Amuck

Personal Notes and Reflections

Lesson Eight

Authority Rides Amuck

Phase 1 -- Inquire:

Supplies:

1) Personality Magic Cards
2) Chart paper and markers

Direct Focus (Objective):

Have the students express their ideas and feelings about authority.

Learning Activities

The instructor facilitates:

1) Break the students into groups of four. Have each behavioral strength (color) represented as clearly as possible in each group: a strong Planner, Builder, Relater and Adventurer. It may be necessary to take the second or even the third strength (color) to make the foursome, if the group tends to be skewed to certain behaviors. Have each group choose a leader.
2) Have each youth give the pros and cons of authority. Have him or her describe the perfect commander in chief. Next, describe at least seven qualities of a person who could be tolerated as a leader. Finally, the qualities shown by a leader who would be disliked and only followed if by force.
3) What is your attitude towards a leader of a gang in contrast to a captain of a team?
4) Pick the leader of your overall group in the following manner. Have all the members pick ONE person from the group with ALL the following three qualifications: a) you are in a crisis situation and you would trust this person with your life. b) You are having a party and this person would be one of the first you would invite. c) You have a serious concern and you would feel confident in sharing it with this same person. Discuss the results of the selection. Mark the name of each person on a piece of paper and tally the results. If there was a single person as a first choice, have that person give a personal reaction to being chosen.
5) Each person, who would like to speak, stands and gives a narrative of his or her "Good-n-New" experience that took place during these activities.
6) Have the teams record their observations on chart paper and report the results to the whole group. Post the charts on the wall for all to see.

Reflection:

1) The Good-n-New for me is ______________________________.
2) Who are the authority figures I like, tolerate and dislike? Why?
3) Was I surprised at the group's choice? If so why, or why not?
4) What facts did you learn about the chosen leader?

Personal Empowerment Statement:

I take pride in being able to carefully choose the persons I follow.

Phase 2 -- Gather:

Supplies:

1) Personality Magic Cards
2) Chart paper and markers
3) ***Harry Potter and the Sorcerer's Stone***

Direct the Focus (Objective):

The students compare and contrast leadership styles

Learning Activities

The instructor facilitates:

A Story for Discussion

Theirs not to make reply, theirs not to reason why,
Theirs but to do and die. Into the valley of Death
Rode the six hundred.
Cannon to the right of them, Cannon to left of them,
Cannon in front of them, Volley'd and thunder'd;
Storm'd at with shot and shell, Boldly they rode and well,
Into the jaws of Death, into the mouth of hell
Rode the six hundred

Alfred Lord Tennyson, *Charge of the Light Brigade*

1) Have the students form the same teams as in the Inquiry stage. However, choose a different leader for each team.
2) A successful leader must be able to bring up the four parts of self: Planner, Builder, Relater or Adventurer, according to the situation. Do you agree or disagree? State the reasons why.
3) Have the teams compare the leadership styles of Albus Dumbledore and Vernon Dursley.
4) List at least seven qualities of Harry Potter's Leadership.
5) Above is a quote from the poem ***"Charge of the Light Brigade"***. Is there such a thing as blind obedience? Discuss the quandary of the soldiers in

Viet Nam, where children and women often carried concealed weapons. Do you shoot woman and children? Should a youth be charged with murder by authorities for shooting and killing classmates?

6) If you were to write a prescription for when and how to use what you have learned from this lesson, what would it be?
7) What was your experience in this class?
8) What new insights did you gain from the activities in this lesson?
9) Each person, who would like to speak, stands and gives a narrative of his or her "Good-n-New" experience that took place during these activities.
10) Have the teams record their observations on chart paper and report the results to the whole group. Post the charts on the wall for all to see.

The Wisdom of the Wizards of the World:

When you come to a fork in the road, take it!

Yogi Berra

Reflection:

1) The Good-n-New for me is ____.
2) My leader style is mainly (Planner, Builder, Relater, Adventurer) __________.
3) The person I choose as a mentor or leader is _______ Why? _____________.

Personal Empowerment Statement:

When I am in a position of leadership, I take pride in knowing the behavioral strengths of those under my command well.

Phase 3 -- Process:

Supplies:

1) Personality Magic Cards
2) Chart paper and markers
3) ***Harry Potter and the Sorcerer's Stone***

Direct the Focus (Objective):

The students discover the power of being a leader

Learning Activities:

The instructor facilitates:

A Story for Discussion

It is interesting to compare the leadership styles of two of the titans of the "high tech" revolution. Steve Jobs would sort the Personality Magic Cards as a Planner (Green) and so would Bill Gates. They both have shown amazing creativity in the founding of Apple and Microsoft, respectively. At one time, there was little to choose between them. From the numerous biographies written about both men, it seems that the Planner Part of Steve Jobs was much stronger than that of Bill Gates. For Jobs, also a strong Adventurer (Red), his focus was on the challenge of creating and improving the "Mac" and leaving the Builder (Brown) activities to others. Gates, on the other hand, had the Builder (Brown) behaviors as a strong backup and capitalized on his creativity with disciplined marketing and organizational skills. The rest is history.

1) Have the students form the same teams as in the Inquiry stage. However, have a different leader for the group.
2) Have them design a chart of the characteristics of excellence expected of a successful leader.
3) Describe Harry Potter as a leader of Hermione Granger and Ron Weasley on their journey through the trap door. (Chapter 16)
4) Did Albus Dumbledore show leadership to Harry Potter? When and in what ways?
5) What changes in perception occurred as a result of the above considerations?
6) Each person, who would like to speak, stands and gives a narrative of his or her "Good-n-New" experience that took place during these activities.
7) Have the teams record their observations on chart paper and report the results to the whole group. Post the charts on the wall for all to see.

The Wisdom of the Wizards of the World:

The letter of the law kills, but the spirit gives life.

New Testament, II Corinthians

Reflection:

1) The Good-n-New for me is ________________________________.
2) Although a successful leader must have all four parts of self-developed, (Planner, Builder, Relater and Adventurer) which behavioral strength do you admire most and why ________________________________.
3) What do you need to do in order to develop leadership qualities?

Personal Empowerment Statement:

When I lead, I take pride in being able to bring up the Planner, Builder, Relater or Adventurer Part of Me as demanded by the situation.

⚒ Phase 4: -- Apply:

Supplies:

1) Personality Magic Cards
2) Chart paper and markers
3) ***Harry Potter and the Sorcerer's Stone***

Direct Focus (Objective):

Students focus in on their particular style of leadership.

Learning Activities

The instructor facilitates:

A Story for Discussion

Our football team had a quarterback who was smart, athletic and capable. He had led the team to two national championships in the previous two years. In his third year, he started to " believe his own press clippings", as they say. In a game or a practice, whenever a play did not go well, he would give his teammates a lecture on their sloppy play or lack of dedication. I had discussed his behavior with him many times, but he persisted. In one particular late season game the team was not doing well and he was getting on everyone's nerves. Midway through the second quarter, his teammates were fed up. They " opened the gates": that is: they didn't block anybody on one play and he was buried by the opposition. We pulled him out of the game and put in the backup quarterback. While we lost the game, he got the message loud and clear and went on to lead the team to a third championship. He learned a valuable lesson in leadership that day.

1) Have the students form the same teams as in the Inquiry stage. Have the final member of the group act as a leader.
2) Identify the leadership style of each member of the group.
3) Invite a respected leader, known by the group, to speak on the power of positive and successful leadership.
4) Each team then examines the leadership style of the person in charge for each of the Phases. Point out the differences of leadership styles.
5) What leadership style (Color) is Professor McGonagall?
6) Have each group write a short, five-minute play, modeling it on Chapter 16. Have Harry, Ron and Hermione represented by members of the group. Be creative and switch parts of the plot. Present the play to the rest of the group.
7) Form conversation circles by having two circles with one circle inside the other. One student from each circle faces another student. In these pairs, students discuss questions that arise from the above experience.
8) Each person, who would like to speak, stands and gives a narrative of his or her "Good-n-New" experience that took place during these activities.

9) Have the teams record their observations on chart paper and report the results to the whole group. Post the charts on the wall for all to see.

The Wisdom of the Wizards of the World:

The final test of a leader is that he leaves behind in other men the conviction and the will to carry on.

Walter Lippmann

Reflection:

1) The Good-n-New for me is ____.
2) Had did I rate as a leader of my group? ______________________________
3) What do I need to do in order to improve my leadership skills? __________

Personal Empowerment Statement:

I get my strength as a leader by choosing well who I follow, thus discovering the needs of a follower.

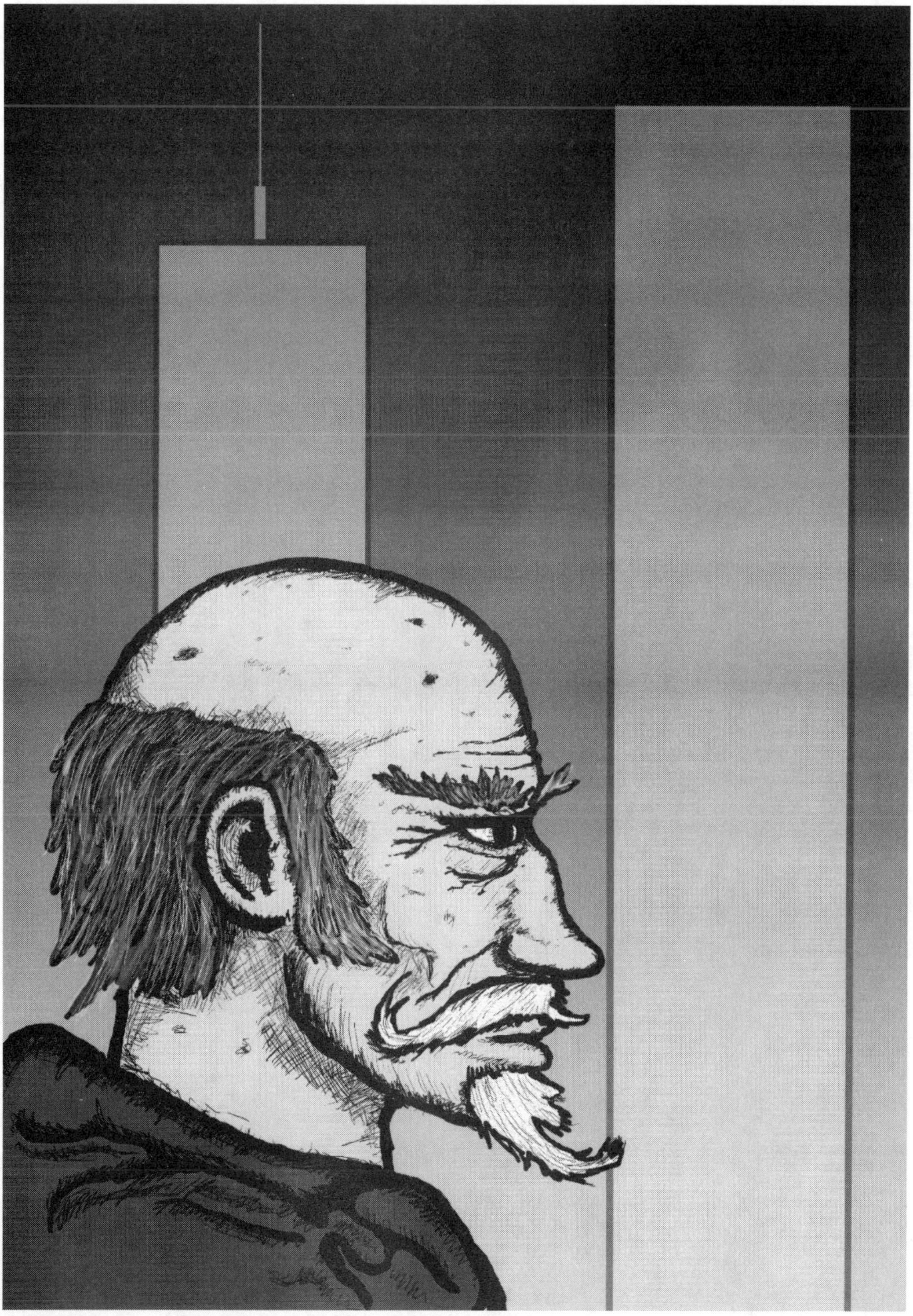

The Eternal Battle Between Good and Evil

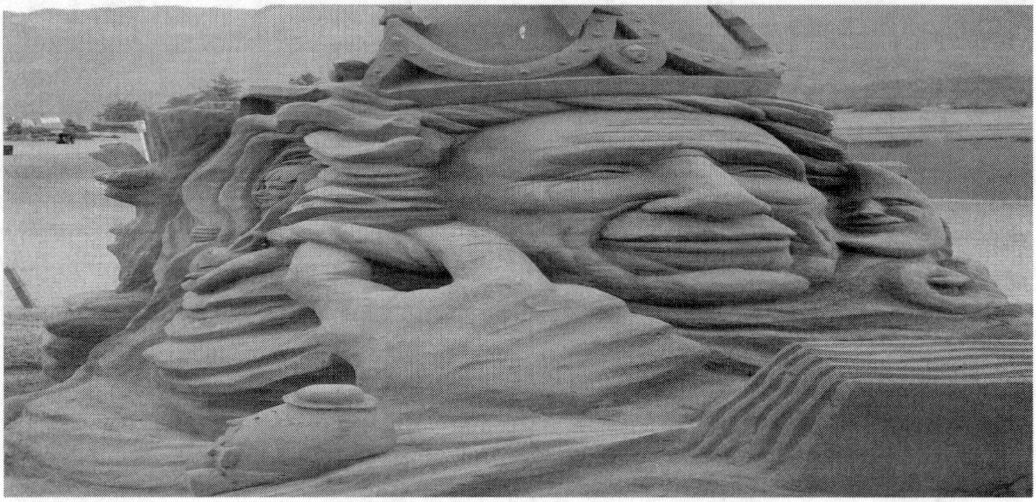

Personal Notes and Reflections

Lesson Nine

The Eternal Battle Between Good and Evil

Phase 1 -- Inquire:

Supplies:

1) Personality Magic Cards
2) Chart paper and markers

Direct Focus (Objective):

Have the students give their interpretation of what is good and evil.

Learning Activities

The instructor facilitates:

1) Break the students into groups of four. Have each behavioral strength (Color) represented as clearly as possible in each group: a strong Planner, Builder, Relater and Adventurer. It may be necessary to take the second or even the third strength (color) to make the foursome, if the group tends to be skewed to certain behaviors.
2) What do I consider evil? What do I consider good? Give examples.
3) What strengths are required to overcome a named evil?
4) What would be the definition of an evil person, versus a good person?
5) Indicate personal encounters containing good or evil situations.
6) Each person, who would like to speak, stands and gives a narrative of his or her "Good-n-New" experience that took place during these activities.
7) Have the teams record their observations on chart paper and report the results to the whole group. Post the charts on the wall for all to see.

Reflection:

1) The Good-n-New for me is ____.
2) Was I surprised at the answers my peers gave in explaining what they thought was good or evil?____

Personal Empowerment Statement:

I take satisfaction in choosing those behaviors required by the situation that are for my personal growth and success in union with the needs of those about me.

Phase 2 -- Gather:

Supplies:

1) Personality Magic Cards
2) Chart paper and markers
3) ***Harry Potter and the Sorcerer's Stone***

Direct the Focus (Objective):

The students define the basic issues involved in distinguishing good from evil.

Lord Voldemort and his followers killed Harry's parents, as well as many good and just persons. Harry was marked with a scar and was saved from death by the love and courage of his mother.
Lord Voldemort could not die, his name, translated from French is "Cheater of death". He always rises up to try and kill his nemesis, Harry. The parallel between Voldemort and terrorists is obvious. **America rises above evil only by the love and courage of its people.** The destruction of the innocent by the terrorists may be halted, but only temporarily, if the necessary precautions are not taken. The price of freedom is vigilance. The challenge for today's youth is the preservation of our way of life, just like it was for generations past. Unlike the past, the battle will take on new forms and faces, but it will always require courage.

A Story for Discussion

On September 11, 2001, one of the most devastating tragedies of American history struck New York City and Washington, D.C. Terrorists struck at the World Trade Center and the Pentagon, with the loss of thousands of innocent lives.

These buildings are the symbols of the Nation's greatest strengths: her business community and her military nerve center. Thomas Aquinas stated that "morality" is the performance of human acts in accordance with right reason. There was no "right reason" in this case. Humans are the only animals endowed with the power of reason. The fact that humans, exercising reason, perpetrated such heinous acts is proof positive that evil does exist. When the grief, the anger and the retribution have passed, evil will still exist. Only by renewing and reinforcing the positive virtues, which have made America the "land of the free and the home of the brave", will we overcome such senseless acts.

1) Have the students form the same teams as in the Inquiry stage.
2) If "good" requires that something that is done must be reasonable, does it mean that all unreasonable actions are evil? Who or what decides what is "unreasonable"?
3) After reading ***Harry Potter and the Sorcerer's Stone,*** do you have a different understanding of good and evil?
4) When Lord Voldemort killed Harry's parents and tried, but failed, to kill Harry, what saved Harry's life?
5) Harry refused to be intimidated by Lord Voldemort. Professor Dumbledore made this clear, when he congratulated Harry for pronouncing the name Voldemort, while others gave up their power to a name. They were so frightened to say it, that he was referred to as "You-Know-Who". (Chapter 17) Is Lord Voldemort evil?
6) Does the term "Terrorist" have the same effect on you as the name of Voldemort has on Harry's friends? Should it?
7) Make a list of great heroic models for us and how, like Harry, they went on a journey of adventure of the struggle between good and evil.
8) Create magic with self-posters, slogans, songs, skits or poetry hailing the power of the inner self. (Each person has at least 12 billion brain cells, each capable of holding two or three million pieces of information.).
9) What new insights did you gain from today's lesson?
10) Each person, who would like to speak, stands and gives a narrative of his or her "Good-n-New" experience that took place during these activities.
11) Have the teams record their observations on chart paper and report the results to the whole group. Post the charts on the wall for all to see.

Wisdom of the Wizards of the World:

Cruelty has a human heart,
And jealousy a human face;
Terror the human form divine,
And secrecy the human dress.

William Blake

Reflection:

1. The Good-n-New for me is ____.
2. Do I take accountability and responsibility for my actions or do I pass the buck? ____

Personal Empowerment Statement:

The power from within me rules my decisions.

Phase 3 -- Process:

Supplies:

1) Personality Magic Cards
2) Chart paper and markers

Direct the Focus (Objective):

The students discover the secret for being an energy giver and not a dead battery.

Learning Activities

The instructor facilitates:

A Story for Discussion

Many years ago, I was a young stockbroker. One day I encountered an older gentleman who had been in the business during the dark days of the stock market crash in 1929. I suggested to him that it must have been a nightmare to be a stockbroker at that time, to which he replied, " Not at all. Remember, every share on the market was selling at bargain prices!" It's all in the way you look at it, I guess.

1) Have the students form the same teams as in the Inquiry stage.
2) Have them describe, to each other, at least one magical aspect of themselves.
3) Do you sometimes meet people who depress you with their presence and others who energize you? Are there energy zappers? Discuss how audiences bring down the energy of an artist or heighten it. Describe any of your own experiences with people who "drain you".
4) What have you learned about yourself in this lesson?
5) Each person, who would like to speak, stands and gives a narrative of his or her "Good-n-New" experience that took place during these activities.

6) Have the teams record their observations on chart paper and report the results to the whole group. Post the charts on the wall for all to see.

Wisdom of the Wizards of the World:

When are you going to get off and stop beating a dead horse?

Evil is wrought by want of Thought
As well as want of Heart

Thomas Hood, *The Lady's Dream*

Reflection:

1) The Good-n-New for me is ______________________________.
2) How do I bring energy to others?______________________________
3) How I zap them and live off the energy of others?______________________________

____

Personal Empowerment Statement:

I am full of energy and seek out others who are go-getters.

Phase 4: -- Apply:

Supplies:

1) Personality Magic Cards
2) Chart paper and markers
3) ***Harry Potter and the Sorcerer's Stone***

Direct the Focus (Objective):

The students teach others what they have learned about the value of positive reality thinking and feeling.

Learning Activities

The instructor facilitates:

A Story for Discussion

Our daughter had a dream of being a vocalist from a very early age. When she was in the third grade, I was reviewing some of her homework with her and noticed that she had signed her name in a couple of places with the letters "stbf" following. When I asked her what they meant, she said, "Soon to be famous!"

1) Have the students form the same teams as in the Inquiry stage.
2) Have the students develop a positive web site, describing concrete, positive behaviors found in ***Harry Potter and the Sorcerer's Stone*** as expressed throughout this text. Set up an explanation program for younger children and their parents using Personality Magic cards and the four phase process as given in each of these chapters.
3) What will you do differently as a result of exploring this lesson on Good versus evil?
4) Is there anything that can be done by this class in preventing terrorism?
5) Discuss how the past cannot be changed and the future is unknown, only the present moment is workable and changeable.
6) Each person, who would like to speak, stands and gives a narrative of his or her "Good-n-New" experience that took place during these activities.
7) Have the teams record their observations on chart paper and report the results to the whole group. Post the charts on the wall for all to see.

Wisdom of the Wizards of the World:

The evil that men do lives after them:
The good is oft interred within their bones.

Shakespeare, *Julius Caesar*

Great heights were reached and kept
By men and women toiling onward in the night!

Adapted from a poem by Alfred Lord Tennyson

Reflection:

1. The Good-n-New for Me is ____.
2. One concrete strategy I will take in describing a beneficial way for others to read ***Harry Potter and the Sorcerer's Stone*** is ________________________.

Personal Empowerment Statement:

My model (name the person) inspires and helps me reach my goals.

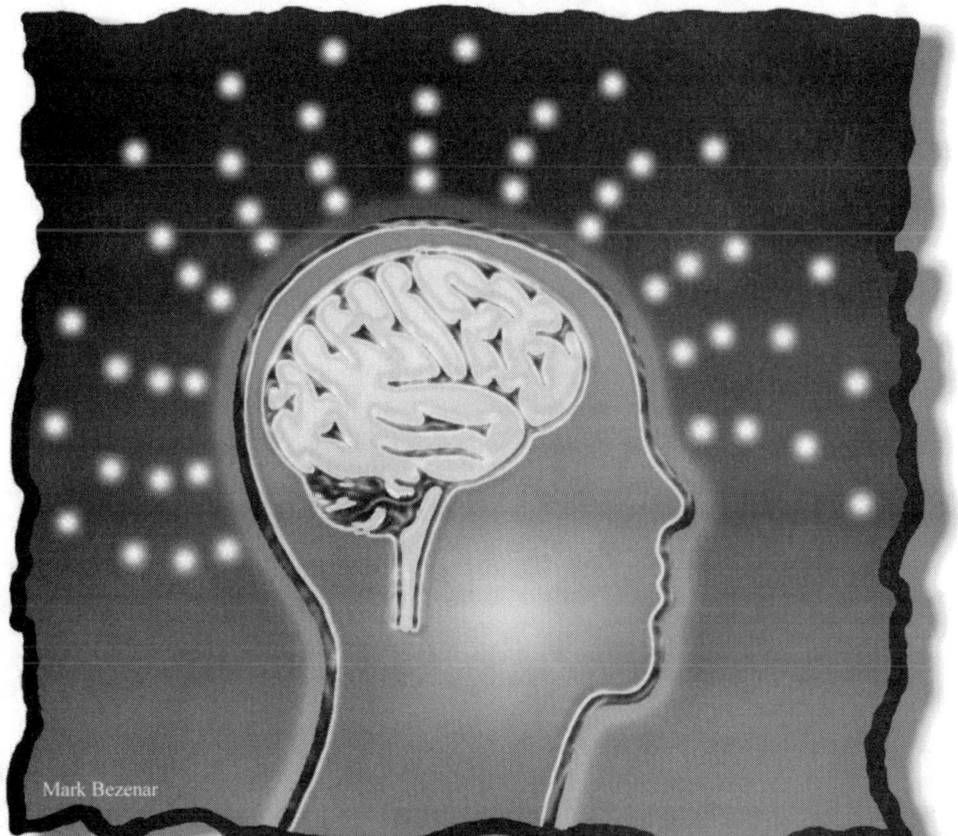

The Quest for Knowledge

Personal Notes and Reflections

Lesson Ten

The Quest for Knowledge

Phase 1 -- Inquire:

Supplies:

1) Personality Magic Cards
2) Chart paper and markers

Direct the Focus (Objective):

The Students identify areas in their lives where they sought out knowledge that led to success.

Learning Activities:

The Instructor facilitates:

1) What happens to your thoughts and feelings when you read Harry Potter? Are you excited, nervous or scared?
2) Play the four corners activity. Place a piece of chart paper, in each corner of the room: on one, place the phrase "Planner – Thinking Part of Me is the Strongest"; on another, "Builder – Leadership Part of Me is the Strongest"; on the third, "Relater – Team Building Part of Me is the Strongest", and; on the last one, "Adventurer – Action Part of Me is the Strongest." Have each youth choose one of the corners and describe her or his success as a Planner, Builder, Relater or Adventurer for two or three minutes. If more than four are in a corner, move some to other corners, based on secondary colors. This may be repeated for the second most successful Part of Self and again for the third. Finally, have them break into the corner of their weakest Part of Self. Have them state why this is the weakest and how they might strengthen this part of self.
3) Another variation of the activity is to place the terms "Academics", "Sports", "Art or Music" and "Relationships" on chart paper in each corner of the room. Have the students go to the corner that they feel represents the Strongest Part of Self. Have each member describe her or his success for two or three minutes. If more than four are in a corner, move some of them to other corners based on secondary colors This may be repeated for the for the second Strongest Part of Self and again for the third.
4) Each person, who would like to speak, stands and gives a narrative of his or her "Good-n-New" experience that took place during these activities.

5) Have the teams record their observations on chart paper and report the results to the whole group. Post the charts on the wall for all to see.

Reflection:

1) The Good-n-New for Me is

____.

2) What have I learned toward strengthening the weakest part of myself?

____

Personal Empowerment Statement:

Take the weakest part of self and make a positive empowerment statement. For example, if the Builder Part of Me is the weakest: "I feel a sense of power in gathering information and making a decision on my own."

Phase 2 -- Gather:

Supplies:

1) Personality Magic Cards
2) Chart paper and markers
3) ***Harry Potter and the Sorcerer's Stone***

Direct the Focus (Objective):

The Students explore the pay value of discovering their strongest learning style and enriching the mind and heart with new creativity.

Learning Activities

The instructor facilitates:

Thoughts for a Discussion

Be careful of your thoughts
For your thoughts become your words.
Be careful of your words
For your words become your actions.
Be careful of your actions
For your actions become your habits.
Be careful of your habits
For your habits become your character.
Be careful of your character
For your character becomes your destiny.

Anonymous

1) Divide the students into groups of four. Have each behavioral strength (color) represented as clearly as possible in each group: a strong Planner, Builder, Relater and Adventurer. It may be necessary to take the second or even the third strength (color) to make the foursome, if the group tends to be skewed to certain behaviors. Choose from the following topics or add your own:
    A) On the chart paper, compare the "nerd" and the "jock". Put the positive and negative aspects for both.
    B) Explore the growth of Hermione Granger from a purely intellectual lifestyle to combining it with the emotional elements of friendship.
    C) Socrates stated "Know Thyself". The most important knowledge is the knowledge of self. Each person in the group writes the highlights of their lives.
2) Check out the learning style of each member in the group. A learning style is the best way that a person may process information. Is it visual, tactile, or auditory? Below is a Learning Styles Map developed by Laurence Martel, Ph.D.

Learning Styles Map

1. Which of the following statements best describes you?
   A. "I remember pictures." B. "I remember what I heard."
   C. "I need to 'feel' or 'act something out' to remember best."
   D. "I remember what I've read."
2. "I work or study best when there is music playing." Yes __ No __
3. "I like dim light to work or study by instead of bright light." Yes __ No __
4. "I like to study/work on a couch or on pillows instead of at a desk." Yes __ No __
5. "I study/work best when I can take little breaks during my work" Yes __ No __
6. "I like to eat or drink while I work." Yes __ No __
7. Which of the following statements best describes you?
   A. "I am a morning person." C. "I am an afternoon person."
   B. "I am a mid-morning person." D. "I am an evening person."
8. The following statement best describes you.
   A. "I like to work alone." C. "I like to work in a group."
   B. "I like to work with a partner."

In question 1, if you answered yes to:
A. You may be a visual learner, who learns best with pictures, diagrams, symbols, etc. You can improve your skills in this area by drawing maps to describe directions or pictures to describe moods and emotions.
B. You may be an auditory learner, who learns best with spoken words or music. You can improve this area by listening to music or lectures and writing or drawing descriptions of what you hear and feel.
C. You may be a kinesthetic learner, who learns best when able to act out, play or be physically involved in what is being learned. Try playing "Charades" to improve your strengths in this area.

D. You may be a print-oriented learner who learns best by reading. Keep a diary, or write often to improve your ability to communicate visually and in print.

Or, you may be a combination of one or more of these. Find out what your strengths and weaknesses are, to better help you succeed.

Questions 2-6. If you answered yes to most of these questions, you may be a global thinker who prefers to get the broad picture and worries less about details or structure. Your vision and what it means to you are most important to your thinking style.
If you answered no to most to these questions, you may be an analytical thinker who prefers details, facts and directions. Your thinking style prefers a step-by-step approach.
Find out your individual style so that you can work your best.
Reproduced with permission from Laurence Martel, Ph.D.
For more information contact The National Academy of Integrative learning,
P.O. Box 5784 Hilton Head SC 29938.
web site: *martel@intellearn.org*

1) Compare the learning styles of Harry Potter and Hermione Granger
2) Explore the wisdom of Professor Dumbledore.
3) Each person, who would like to speak, stands and gives a narrative of his or her "Good-n-New" experience that took place during these activities.
4) Have the teams record their observations on chart paper and report the results to the whole group. Post the charts on the wall for all to see.

Wisdom of the Wizards of the World:

Good nature and good sense must ever join;
To err is human, to forgive divine.

Pope, *Essay on Criticism*

Errors, like straws, upon the surface flow;
He who would search for pearls must dive below.

Dryden, *All for Love,* Prologue

Reflection:

1) The Good-n-New for me is ________________________________.
2) What is the easiest way for me to process information (learning style)?
3) Why are my studies important for me? List the reasons.

Personal Empowerment Statement:

I have a thrill in discovering new ideas and creatively using my talents (list, for example: music, science, math, chemistry, carpentry, art).

Phase 3 -- Process:

Supplies:

1) Personality Magic Cards
2) Chart paper and markers

Direct the Focus (Objective):

The students learn to appreciate the value of knowledge and their particular way of processing information.

Learning Activities

The instructor facilitates:

A Story for Discussion

Our son is a true Adventurer (Red). When he was in grade 3, the teacher gave him this note to take home to his parents:

" 9:07 AM: John has finally settled down to his desk
9:14 AM: John is acting rather fidgety
9:17 AM: John has just used 2 ½ minutes to sharpen his pencil
9:20 AM: John has settled down again
9:41 AM: John is looking around the class to see what everyone else is doing.
9:56 AM: John is now picking his nose
10:07 AM: John has gone to sharpen an already sharp pencil
10:15 AM: John has just tugged on Billy's shirt
10:20 AM: John has pushed himself into the front of the line at recess.
I would like to meet with you to discuss this!"

The teacher was a Builder (Brown) who insisted on discipline, order and decorum in the classroom. At the meeting, the teacher suggested that John, and his friend Billy, were unable to learn and should be transferred to special needs classes. John is now President of a multinational technology company and Billy is a football coach at a Midwestern University. The teacher felt that there was only one effective learning style. As a corollary, another son attended the same teacher's class the following year and introduced himself to the teacher with: " I just want you to know, I am not my brother."

A teacher should have maximum authority and minimal power.
Thomas Szasz, *the second sin "Education"*

Beethoven's music teacher once said of him, "As a composer, he is hopeless."

1) Have the students form the same teams as the Gather stage.
2) On the chart paper, have each group list all the ideas and feelings that they experienced in the exercises of this text on the chart paper. Have each

member of the group give at least one new insight. Each group reports back their list and posts it for all to see.

3) Have members of the group write slogans, poetry, skits, posters or a short story highlighting his and her particular insight.
4) Have the students make a list of Negative Put Downs they have experienced. Opposite each Put Down place a Positive Put Up statement.
5) Each person, who would like to speak, stands and gives a narrative of his or her "Good-n-New" experience that took place during these activities.
6) Have the teams record their observations on chart paper and report the results to the whole group. Post the charts on the wall for all to see.

Wisdom of the Wizards of the World:

The window is not the view; the window allows the view.

Hugh Prather

Inch-by-Inch, It Is a Cinch

Rev. Robert Schuller

Reflection:

1) The Good-n-New for me is ________________________________.
2) Who and which idea impressed and is of personal value to me?__________

Personal Empowerment Statement:

I appreciate the opportunity to learn at least one new exciting idea each day.

Phase 4: -- Apply:

Supplies:

1) Personality Magic Cards
2) Chart paper and markers

Direct the Focus (Objective):

Open the student's minds to "Possibility Thinking".

Learning Activities

The instructor facilitates:

Thoughts for Discussion

To be nobody but yourself – in a world which is doing its best – to make you everybody else – means to fight the hardest battle which any human can fight, and never stop fighting.

E. E. Cummings

1) Have the students form the same teams as in the Gather stage.
2) Play the song "The Impossible Dream" or similar song. Make a list of at least 50 goals or dreams that you wish to accomplish in your lifetime.
3) Read or watch the film *The Man from La Mancha.* (Don Quixote)
4) The poets have described the quest for knowledge in many ways: "A little learning is a dangerous thing;" " Drink deep or taste not the Pierian

Spring!" Search out and list other quotes expressing the value of knowledge.

5) Discuss the possibility of having a mentor or experienced guide in your area of special interest. For example, if your interest is writing, a successful author, in business, a successful businessperson, or in relationships, a person who is excellent in relating with others. List mentors who you admire and could help you personally develop your talents.
6) Each person, who would like to speak, stands and gives a narrative of his or her "Good-n-New" experience that took place during these activities.
7) Have the teams record their observations on chart paper and report the results to the whole group. Post the charts on the wall for all to see.

Wisdom of the Wizards of the World:

If my theory of relativity is proven successful, Germany will claim me, as a German and France will declare that I am a citizen of the world. Should my theory prove untrue, France will say that I am a German and Germany will declare that I am a Jew.

Albert Einstein, Address, *at the Sorbonne*

Reflection:

1) The Good-n-New for me is ________________________________.
2) Who would be a good mentor for me? ________________________
(If there is not one to your knowledge, goal set to find one.)

Personal Empowerment Statement:

I desire with all my heart, body and mind to find a person knowledgeable and caring, who would be able to counsel me in (list the area you would like guidance).

MONSTERS UNDER THE BED

Personal Notes and Reflections

Lesson Eleven

Monsters Under the Bed

Phase 1 -- Inquire:

Supplies:

1) Personality Magic Cards
2) Chart paper and markers

Direct the Focus (Objective):

The students describe and examine their fears and why they have them.

Learning Activities

The instructor facilitates:

1) Break the students into groups of four. Have each behavioral strength (color) represented as best as possible in each group: a strong Planner, Builder, Relater and Adventurer. It may be necessary to take the second or even the third strength (color) to make the foursome, if the group tends to be skewed to certain behaviors.
2) Have the students make a list of what scares them on the chart paper. Include the reasons why they feel scared.
3) Each person, who would like to speak, stands and gives a narrative of his or her "Good-n-New" experience that took place during these activities.
4) Have the teams record their observations on chart paper and report the results to the whole group. Post the charts on the wall for all to see.

Reflection:

1) The Good-n-New for me is ______________________________.
2) List what scares me and why.

Personal Empowerment Statement:

I have the power within me to say no and stand up for my beliefs when I (Name the fear situation and strategy to overcome the fear). Do not mention fear in the statement but the positive cure, as the mind works on the concrete level, with whatever you tell it. For example: "I have the power within me to say no and stand up for my beliefs when I refuse to smoke a cigarette when pressure is put on me by (name of the person)."

☎ Phase 2 -- Gather:

Supplies:

1) Personality Magic Cards
2) Chart paper and markers
3) ***Harry Potter and the Sorcerer's Stone***

Direct the Focus (Objective):

Have the students explore other options, other than being victimized by fear.

Learning Activities

The instructor facilitates:

A Story for Discussion

The "greatest fear is fear itself." During the Second World War, during the bombing of London and Pearl Harbor, fear was rampant. As Winston Churchill and Roosevelt led the allies, the greatest obstacle to overcome was the fear of defeat. They knew that fear is the first step to defeat and being conquered. The Nazis particularly, used the media as a fear tool, both to conquer and control their own people and to frighten the allies into accepting defeat.

1) Divide the students into groups of four. Have each behavioral strength (color) represented as clearly as possible in each group: a strong Planner, Builder, Relater and Adventurer. It may be necessary to take the second or even the third strength (color) to make the foursome, if the group tends to be skewed to certain behaviors.
2) Only Harry has no fear to speak Lord Voldemort's name. All the rest say, "You-know-who." What does this mean to you? Discuss how power is delegated to things outside you, whether it is a name, object (walking under a ladder) or person (teacher, peer). Have the youths list the situations when this power is given outside self. Indicate the positive and negative effects.
3) Make posters, skits or songs having power over the person.
4) List some of the "monsters" that are friends of Hagrid. How does this apply to the your life situations? Name some of the monsters in your life.
5) What is a nightmare? Describe one.
6) What about Nearly Headless Nick and the other ghosts? What power do ghosts have over your life? Why is it frightening for some people to go into a graveyard at night?
7) Discuss how the terror created by the destruction of the twin towers may change a person's life for better or worse?
8) What happened to your thoughts and feelings as you conclude this lesson?
9) What new insights did you gain from this lesson?

10) Each person, who would like to speak, stands and gives a narrative of his or her "Good-n-New" experience that took place during these activities.
11) Have the teams record their observations on chart paper and report the results to the whole group. Post the charts on the wall for all to see.

Wisdom of the Wizards of the World:

It is hard to fight an enemy who has outposts in your head.

Sally Kempton

Reflection:

1) The Good-n-New for me is ________________________________.
2) What are my personal fears and how might I control or even overcome them so they do not have power over my life?

Personal Empowerment Statement:

I feel courageous, in complete control and full of energy when (describe the strategy to overcome the fear). For example: when I stand up to speak in front of (name the group, person or situation).

Phase 3 -- Process:

Supplies:

1) Personality Magic Cards
2) Chart paper and markers
3) ***Harry Potter and the Sorcerer's Stone***

Direct the Focus (Objective):

Have the students come to terms with their fears.

Learning Activities

The instructor facilitates:

A Tale for Discussion

C-A-N-C-E-R is a monster in any language. My sister was given this diagnosis. It was a powerful blow to the whole family. We were at odds as to what should be said or done. We felt she had been handed the death sentence. When we would see her, we talked about everything but the "word". It was a word no one wanted to hear or speak. Fortunately for us, she felt she had to talk about it and demanded we talk about cancer. The word "cancer" to us today is just a word that we are allowed to say because she took the power away from the word. She put it in its proper perspective. Her strong positive attitude had helped us all. She continued to receive her treatments and today is stronger emotionally and physically. So are we.

1) Break the students into groups of four. Have each behavioral strength (color) represented as clearly as possible in each group: a strong Planner, Builder, Relater and Adventurer. It may be necessary to take the second or even the third strength (color) to make the foursome, if the group tends to be skewed to certain behaviors.
2) Take them on a creative mind journey. The following is called the flip back, flip up technique. The basis is that the mind can shift much faster than the emotions. The objective is to carry over the good feeling to overcome the negative image.
   Have the students imagine they are a rock in the middle of a stream and the water is rushing past them. Have them repeat, "I am a rock, I am rock". Once they have reached a feeling of power and control, have them imagine the fear (for example a spider, a person, a snake) being swept on past them in the rushing water. If the fear starts to come back, return to the image of the rock. Repeat, " I am a rock, I am a rock".
3) Have the students ask themselves if they have an emotional attachment to a certain fear. What could be the reasons (a bad experience such as a car crash and fear of riding in a car; forgotten, suppressed memories)?
4) Discuss common fears, such as speaking in front of a group and fear of the dark. How did Harry overcome his fears?
5) Are there legitimate fears that need precautions? What may some of them be? Make positive posters of fears being conquered.
6) Each person, who would like to speak, stands and gives a narrative of his or her "Good-n-New" experience that took place during these activities.
7) Have the teams record their observations on chart paper and report the results to the whole group. Post the charts on the wall for all to see.

Wisdom of the Wizards of the World:

Courage is fear holding on a minute longer.

George Patton

Reflection:

1) The Good-n-New for me is ______________________________.
2) What legitimate fears should I take heed and have strategies? List them.

Personal Empowerment Statement:

I take powerful precautions and develop strategies for handling fearful situations (name) or people (name).

⚒ Phase 4: -- Apply:

Supplies:

1) Personality Magic Cards
2) Chart paper and markers

Direct the Focus (Objective):

The students create strategies for handling both legitimate and illegitimate fears in a positive and successful way.

Learning Activities

The instructor facilitates:

A Tale for Discussion

As late as the end and beginning of the 20th century in merry old England, those with mental challenges where locked up and put on show for monetary gain in a pit. Then Sigmund Freud discovered the following: A young lady went into hysterics whenever she took up a glass of water to drink. Through analysis, he took her back to her early childhood. She had lived with her grandmother who had many cats. She would let the cats drink out of a glass and then give it to the young lady to finish. Her grandmother was the authority figure, so even though the young lady found it repulsive, she drank from the glass anyway. As the years progressed the experience grew, hidden in her mind, until drinking water from a glass finally made her feel hysterical.

1) Ask the students to individually write out up to three legitimate fears they have and three phony fears that are trumped up in the imagination. Now, have them draw up strategies for dealing positively and concretely with them. Have them make posters, cartoons, slogans, poems or empowerment statements showing the defeat of dangers real or imagined.
2) Have a trust walk in the room. Break into partners; one blindfolded, the other not blindfolded. Place obstacles around the room that the blindfolded person is not aware of. Have the partner lead the blindfolded person through the maze. Change partners and repeat with a different configuration for the maze.
3) Have a brainstorm session. Team members take turns adding to a group brainstorm.
4) What have you learned from this lesson?
5) Each person, who would like to speak, stands and gives a narrative of his or her "Good-n-New" experience that took place during these activities.

6) Have the partners record their observations on chart paper and report the results to the whole group. Post the charts on the wall for all to see.

Wisdom of the Wizards of the World:

Tell me and I may forget.
Show me and I may remember.
Involve me and I will understand.

Anonymous

Reflection:

1) The Good-n-New for me is ________________________________.
2) What is most important imaginary fear that I need to take steps to control and conquer?________________________________
3) What is most important real fear that I need to take steps to control and conquer?________________________________

Personal Empowerment Statement:

I have the strength to conquer and successfully handle (name fear person or situation)

*** Note that when the fear is great, it is beneficial to imagine a successful and positive feeling from the past. The **feeling** of the positive experience must be strong and vivid to have success. When this feeling is at its height, switch the imagination to handling the fear of the person or situation. As soon as the fear starts to return, switch back to the positive experience. When one is able to visualize the person or situation in a positive manner, so will it become true in reality. The basis for this strategy is that emotions linger longer than an image. A transfer is changing the fear feeling to a positive feeling of control and success. If everything else fails, do it and you can replace fear with a successful positive constructive strategy.

Celebrate Life

Personal Notes and Reflections

Chapter Twelve

Celebrate Life

Phase 1 -- Inquire:

Supplies:

1) Personality Magic Cards
2) Chart paper and markers

Direct the Focus (Objective):

The students examine their own positive group celebration experiences and the feelings connected with them.

Learning Activities

The instructor facilitates:

1) Break the students into groups of four. Have each behavioral strength (color) represented as clearly as possible in each group: a strong Planner, Builder, Relater and Adventurer. It may be necessary to take the second or even the third strength (color) to make the foursome, if the group tends to be skewed to certain behaviors.
2) Have the students list the feasts or celebrations in their lives and the experiences connected with them
3) What were you thinking and feeling about during this activity?
4) Each person, who would like to speak, stands and gives a narrative of his or her "Good-n-New" experience that took place during these activities.
5) Have the teams record their observations on chart paper and report the results to the whole group. Post the charts on the wall for all to see.

Reflection:

1) The Good-n-New for me is ______________________________.
2) What is the celebration that I remember most? ______________________

Personal Empowerment Statement:

I take great pleasure in bringing up my super positive feelings and memory of (name the celebration) to uplift me, often.

Phase 2 -- Gather:

Supplies:

1) Personality Magic Cards
2) Chart paper and markers
3) ***Harry Potter and the Sorcerer's Stone***

Direct the Focus (Objective):

The students come to realize the power of celebrating life not just on holidays.

Learning Activities

The instructor facilitates:

A Story for Discussion

We recently attended the wedding of the daughter of a friend. The bride was gorgeous in her ornate gown and the groom and groomsmen looked resplendent. The church was beautifully decorated and the service was both tasteful and joyful. It was followed by an elegant reception, after which the bride and groom were carried away in a horse-drawn carriage.

I also remember the day I graduated from University. My wife and I got a babysitter, went out for Pizza with wine and then went to see an English comedy movie. That is the celebration I will remember long after the wedding has faded.

1) Have the students form the same teams as in the Inquiry stage.
2) Consider the celebrations in ***Harry Potter and the Sorcerer's Stone***. Compare the content and focus of the celebrations at the Dursleys, such as Dudley's birthday, to the celebrations at Hogwarts and Harry's participation. List them and write them out.
3) What are at least seven ingredients in making a successful celebration?
4) What influenced your thoughts and feelings during the above activities?
5) Each person, who would like to speak, stands and gives a narrative of his or her "Good-n-New" experience that took place during these activities.
6) Have the teams record their observations on chart paper and report the results to the whole group. Post the charts on the wall for all to see.

Wisdom of the Wizards of the World:

The man who has no inner life is the slave of his own surroundings.

Henri Frederic Amiel

Reflection:

1) The Good-n-New for me is ______________________________.
2) Were you surprised at the different ways the persons in the group celebrate? If so, why? ______________________________

Personal Empowerment Statement:

I get pleasure from and benefit from setting up even a small celebration for those I care for when they (name) least expect it.

Phase 3 -- Process:

Supplies:

1) Personality Magic Cards
2) Chart paper and markers
3) ***Harry Potter and the Sorcerer's Stone***

Direct the Focus (Objective):

Have the students determine the reasons for celebrating life other than on traditional dates such Anniversaries, New Years and Birthdays.

Learning Activities

The instructor facilitates:

A Tale for Discussion

During my younger years I was part of a group of about 30 persons for a year. Each 25th of the month, we celebrated Christmas. Hand-made presents were given to designate others so all received one gift. There were songs and decorations combined with meals fit for a king. What was particularly effective: there was no commercialism, only the satisfaction and joy of celebrating life as a family.

1) Have the students form the same teams as in the Inquiry stage.
2) Ask them to focus on the following questions
    A) What is the reason and purpose of celebrating?
    B) What is the history of days that most people celebrate now?
    C) What are the benefits of celebrating with others?
3) As a group, write an overview of Hogwarts celebrations: mealtimes, the arrival of the mail and decorations. Describe the atmosphere of the celebrations.
4) As a group, write a description of the meals at Hogwarts compared with those at the Dursley's.
5) Each person, who would like to speak, stands and gives a narrative of his or her "Good-n-New" experience that took place during these activities.
6) Have the teams record their observations on chart paper and report the results to the whole group. Post the charts on the wall for all to see.

Wisdom of the Wizards of the World:

Hitch your wagon to a star.

Emerson, *Civilization*

Reflection:

1) The Good-n-New for me is ____.
2) What is of personal benefit in a Life Celebration?

Personal Empowerment Statement:

1) I enjoy making people (name) happy on a day I choose to Celebrate Life.
2) Make and write out other empowerment statements of value to me.

Phase 4 -- Apply:

Supplies:

1) Personality Magic Cards
2) Chart paper and markers
3) ***Harry Potter and the Sorcerer's Stone***

Direct the Focus (Objective):

The students consider the value of living life to its fullest at the present moment.

Learning Activities

The instructor facilitates:

A Tale for Discussion

My mentor is responsible for a great part of my thinking. He always emphasized the value of living the present moment to its fullest. The past is past so let the dead bury the dead. The future has not yet come and, to a great degree, it is beyond our control. We only have the present moment and the responsibility to use that moment to its fullest, as "we cannot go home again".

1) Have the students form the same teams as in the Inquiry stage.
2) Compare your view of life and how it should be lived to how Harry Potter lived his.

3) Have a CELEBRATION OF LIFE party. Draw cartoons and posters, write poems, slogans and perform a skit that highlights the celebration. Have the students bring in a small gift for a designated other, less than 50 cents in value and preferably hand made by the person. Decorate the room and have singsongs and games. Have the teams gather at the end to debrief the experience.
4) Team creates a cheer for the group to be used when the group has accomplished a task and is celebrating.
5) Using a large sheet of paper, create a mind map of the 12 lessons: a form of brainstorming using a free-flowing documentation process, where lines connect concepts to each other. The core subject, Character Education, is in the center; the main spokes are the lessons. Have the students indicate related ideas. These can be color coded, circled or attached by lines. Pictures and words can both be used.
6) Teams produce a product or engage in a project as a culminating activity.
7) Teams prepare a performance or presentation based on a synthesis of what they have learned in the twelve lessons.
8) Each team selects a food (vegetable, fruit, gum, fruit or vegetable drink, ice-cream, chocolate milk) that the whole group enjoys and can be used in a class celebration.
9) Each person, who would like to speak, stands and gives a narrative of his or her "Good-n-New" experience that took place during these activities.
10) Have the teams record their observations on chart paper and report the results to the whole group. Post the charts on the wall for all to see.

Wisdom of the Wizards of the World:

There is a time to let things happen and a time to make things happen.

Hugh Prather

Reflection:

1) The Good-n-New for me is ____.
2) How often would it be beneficial for me to Celebrate Life?

Personal Empowerment Statement:

I take pride and feel great in being able to bring up joy and fun into my own life and others (name and date).

Bibliography

Neilson, Stefan. *Personality Magic, I See What You are Thinking,* (Booklet) Seattle: Aeon Hierophant Publishing, 2001

Neilson, Stefan & Thoelke, Shay. *Careers Unlimited, To Be or Not to Be,* Seattle: Aeon Hierophant Publishing, 1999

Neilson, Stefan & Thoelke, Shay. *Conflict Resolution Through Winning Colors®* Seattle: Aeon Hierophant Publishing, 1999

Neilson, Stefan & Thoelke, Shay. *Here's Looking at You Kid!* (Coil Bound) Seattle: Aeon Hierophant Publishing, 1988

Neilson, Stefan & Thoelke, Shay. *Leadership, Team Building, Self-esteem and Conflict Resolution Communication,* (Coil Bound) Seattle: Aeon Hierophant Publishing, 1998

Neilson, Stefan & Thoelke, Shay. *Winning Professionally and Personally,* Seattle: Aeon Hierophant Publishing, 2001

Prather, Hugh. *Notes on Love and Courage.* New York: Doubleday Company, Inc., 1977

Rowling, J. K. *Harry Potter and the Sorcerer's Stone.* New York: Scholastic Inc., 1998

Thoelke, Shay. *Service Learning Team Community Experience Using Winning Colors® in an Elementary School, Level One,* (Coil Bound) Seattle: Aeon Hierophant Publishing, 2001

Thoelke, Shay. *Service Learning Team Community Experience Using Winning Colors® in a Middle School, Level Two,* (Coil Bound) Seattle: Aeon Hierophant Publishing, 2001

Thoelke, Shay. *Service Learning Team Community Experience Using Winning Colors®, Level Three,* (Coil Bound) Seattle: Aeon Hierophant Publishing, 2001

Williams, R. Bruce & Dunn, Steven E. *Brain Compatible Learning for the Block.* Arlington Heights, Illinois: Skylight Professional Development, 2000

The "mindkey" illustration
is symbolic of a person's quest
to find the key to his and her own mind
that will unlock his and her potential.
As with Harry Potter at the outset,
many people are not aware
of the power and potential they possess.
Much of the struggle, enchantment and
reward in life are related to this search for
personal power, understanding and
awareness.

Those Parents and Teachers who wish to use the *Sorcerer's Stone* for positive behavioral character development rather than just entertainment will find *Character Education: The Legacy of the Harry Potter Novels* crucial.

Ten chapters, dealing with essential behaviors for positive character development, are found in the novel: Friendship, Spoiled Child, Captain Courageous, False Judgments, Child Abuse and Bullies, Model Adventurer, Authority, Battle of Good and Evil, Quest for Knowledge, Monsters Under the Bed and Celebrating Life.
Tools such as an Inquire, Gather, Process and Apply paradigm plus a learning styles indicator and a set of communication cards are included.

Name: ______________________ e-mail for updates ____________________

Address: ____

City: ____________________ State _____ Zip: __________ Phone: (_____) ___________

Character Education: The Legacy of Harry Potter $ 29.95 (Includes a free set of communication cards.
Check/money order enclosed: _________

Personal and Financial Success, Inc. P. O. Box 96, Mountlake Terrace WA 98043 (425) 672-8222
e-mail: winningcolors@mindspring.com Web sites: winningcolors.com & financialsuccessinc.com

Investment		Number	Total
Character Education: The Legacy of Harry Potter	$ 29.95	______	$ _____
Audio Tape by Random House (Performance by Jim Dale):			
Harry Potter and the Sorcerer's Stone	$ 35.00	______	$ _____
Harry Potter and the Chamber of Secrets	$ 35.00	______	$ _____
Harry Potter and the Prisoner of Azkaban	$ 35.00	______	$ _____
Harry Potter and the Goblet of Fire	$ 39.95	______	$ _____
CD by Random House (Performance by Jim Dale):			
Harry Potter and the Sorcerer's Stone	$ 49.95	______	$ _____
Harry Potter and the Chamber of Secrets	$ 49.95	______	$ _____
Harry Potter and the Prisoner of Azkaban	$ 54.95	______	$ _____
Harry Potter and the Goblet of Fire	$ 69.95	______	$ _____

Add $ 2.00 Mail (Priority Mail $ 3.90) Total Investment ________

Name: ______________________________ e-mail for updates ____________________

Address: ____ City: ____________________

State _____ Zip: ____________ Phone: (_____) __________________ P.O. # ___________

Personal and Financial Success, Inc. P. O. Box 96, Mountlake Terrace WA 98043
(425) 672-8222 e-mail: winningcolors@mindspring.com
Web sites: winningcolors.com & financialsuccessinc.com

WINNING COLORS® CARD SETS

Quant.	Price	Catalog #	Description
_____	$10.00	E700	Modern Communication Card set, teen **(NEW)**
_____	$12.00	E700L	Modern Communication Card set, laminated **(NEW)**
_____	$10.00	B701	Modern Communication Card set, adult **(NEW)**
_____	$12.00	C201L	Modern Communication Card set, Adult, laminated **(NEW)**
_____	$10.00	C300	Traditional Card set, elementary to lower middle school
_____	$12.00	C301L	Traditional Card set, elementary to lower middle school, laminated
_____	$10.00	C200	Traditional Card set, middle school or lower reading level
_____	$12.00	C201L	Traditional Card set, middle school or lower reading level, laminated
_____	$10.00	C100US	Traditional Card set, U.S. adult
_____	$12.00	C101USL	Traditional Card set, U.S. adult, laminated
_____	$10.00	C500AUS	Card set, Australian adult
_____	$12.00	C501AUSL	Card set, Australian adult, laminated
_____	$10.00	C600CAN	Card set, Canadian adult
_____	$12.00	C601CANL	Card set, Canadian adult, laminated
_____	$10.00	C600CANT	Card set, Canadian teen
_____	$12.00	C601CANTL	Card set, Canadian teen, laminated
_____	$10.00	C400S	Card set, teen to adult Spanish
_____	$12.00	C401SL	Card set, teen to adult Spanish, laminated

WINNING COLORS® PUBLICATIONS FOR EDUCATION AND BUSINESS

Quant.	Price	Catalog #	Description
_____	$29.95	Success	Winning Professionally and Personally **(NEW)**
_____	$29.95	HP	Character Education: The Harry Potter Legacy **(NEW)**
_____	$19.95	Booklet	Booklet containing cards and crucial explanations for presenters **(NEW)**
_____	$19.95	43KID	"Here's Looking at You, Kid: K-3" Reproduction rights available
_____	$29.95	43KIDI	Instructor's manual for 43KID above
_____	$19.95	41ELEM	Winning Colors Power Pack for elementary students
_____	$29.95	42ELEMI	Includes 41ELEM Winning Colors® Power Pack for instructors
_____	$19.95	31T	Leadership, Team Building, Self-esteem, Conflict Resolution Power Pack
_____	$29.95	32TI	Instructor's manual (includes 31T) grades 6-8 or lower reading levels)
_____	$19.95	37HS	Leadership, Team Building, Self-esteem, Conflict Resolution Power Pack
_____	$29.95	38HSI	Instructor's manual (includes 37HS) High School to University level
_____	$95.00	OVER1	Transparency Masters, detailed instructions for instructors

_____	$19.95	21E	Leadership, Team Building, Self-esteem, Conflict Resolution Power Pack
_____	$29.952	2EI	Instructor's manual (includes 21E) —adult level
_____	$19.952	1ECAN	Leadership, Team Building, Self-esteem, Conflict Resolution Power Pack Canadian edition
_____	$29.95	22EICAN	Instructors manual (includes 21ECAN) adult level, Canadian
_____	$24.95	1ENER	Energizing the Internet of the Brain
_____	$29.95	ICONFCB	Conflict Resolution Through Winning Colors (Coil Bound)
_____	$29.95	ICONFPB	Conflict Resolution Through Winning Colors (Paperback)
_____	$29.951	ICARECB	Careers Unlimited; To Be or Not To Be (Coil Bound)
_____	$29.951	ICAREPB	Careers Unlimited; To Be or Not To Be (Paperback))
_____	$17.951	THOT	Thoughts of the Seasons: A Journey Through the Colors
_____	$29.95	SERV1	Service Learning Level One (Elementary)
_____	$29.9	5SERV2	Service Learning Level Two (Intermediate)
_____	$29.95	SERV3	Service Learning Level Three (Community at Large)
_____	$49.00	VIDEO1	Leadership, Team Building, Self-esteem, Conflict Resolution Power Pack - Teen-University hands-on communication video
_____	$89.95	VIDEO2	Instructor's Video. Spontaneous classroom presentation by several instructors to high school students.
_____	$49.95	OCEAN	Beautiful scenic background video for presentations and relaxation (**NEW**)
_____	$19.95	Music CD	Music and songs for each of the colors
_____	$19.95	Music Tape	Music and songs for each of the colors

Name: ______________________ e-mail for updates ______________________

Address: ______________________________ City: ______________________

State _____ Zip: __________ Phone: (_____) ______________ P.O. # ______________

Character Education: The Legacy of Harry Potter $ 29.95 (Includes a set of communication cards.
Check/money order enclosed: _________)

Personal and Financial Success, Inc. P. O. Box 96, Mountlake Terrace WA 98043 (425) 672-8222
e-mail: winningcolors@mindspring.com Web sites: winningcolors.com & financialsuccessinc.com